MW00698134

PROTECTIVE OPTIONS STRATEGIES

MARRIED PUTS AND COLLAR SPREADS

ERNIE ZERENNER & MICHAEL CHUPKA

Marketplace Books
Columbia, Maryland

Publisher: Chris Myers
VP/General Manager: John Boyer
Executive Editor: Jody Costa
Development Editor: Courtney Jenkins
Art Director: Larry Strauss
Graphic Designer: Jennifer Marin
Production Designer: Becki Choi

Copyright © 2008 by Michael Chupka & Ernie Zerenner

Published by Marketplace Books Inc.

All rights reserved.

Reproduction or translation of any part of this work beyond that permitted by section 107 or 108 of the 1976 United States Copyright Act without the permission of the copyright owner is unlawful. Requests for permission or further information should be addressed to the Permissions Department at Marketplace Books®.

This publication is designed to provide accurate and authoritative information in regard to the subject matter covered. It is sold with the understanding that neither the author nor the publisher is engaged in rendering legal, accounting, or other professional service. If legal advice or other expert assistance is required, the services of a competent professional person should be sought.

From a Declaration of Principles jointly adopted by a Committee of the American Bar Association and a Committee of Publishers.

ISBN: 1-59280-342-3

ISBN 13: 978-1-59280-342-2

Printed in the United States of America.

TABLE OF CONTENTS

INTRODUCTION

There are many different types of people in the world and each one has his own personal beliefs, goals, ideals, ideas, dreams, and ambitions. There are risk takers and risk avoiders; goal driven and goal oriented individuals; day dreamers and quiet dreamers; optimists and pessimists; those who reach for the stars and those who keep their feet firmly planted on the ground; those that live for the moment and those that plan for a potentially more stable future.

Every day there are countless subjects, concepts, and situations that present themselves, each event a boon or bump along our road of life. For every topic that presents itself there are just as many solutions that cover every broad philosophy; from those that exist at both extremes of a never-ending spectrum, to all the possibilities that fall in between.

Psychologists and philosophers will tell us that the way in which we choose to deal with each scenario will define our character and personality. Are you are a risk taker? Are you a risk avoider? Do you work to achieve goals? Do you dream and hope that your goals will come to fruition? Is your glass half empty, or is it half full?

As you choose in life, so you choose to invest.

That being said, we have to agree on certain truths, despite any individual differences we might have on politics or policy. Disregarding the clichés of death and taxes as obvious references to certain truths, we want to focus on the truths of a growing and expanding economy.

"What growing and expanding economy?" you might question. With all the concerns and daily media attention about the housing and credit crisis, the increasing gas prices that loom over our heads, and when it seems that all profitable companies are outsourcing jobs overseas, how can we possibly agree on the so called truth of a growing economy?

History shows that the economy as a whole is a growth investment. The population is ever expanding, ergo the workforce is ever expanding. Does not growth and expansion follow an expanding workforce? The natural bias is for the market to go up, typically about 10% per year. As investors, we know this is not always the case. What goes up must come down. Expansive growth cannot exist without the occasional decline.

So what is an investor to do, knowing that historically the market is expanding and growing, but there are times when the market must fall? Can an investor look to be a risk taker while at the same time be a risk avoider? Can an investor be an optimist and put their money into proven growth stocks while at the same time protect the investment against unforeseen pessimism? Can the glass be half empty, but at the same time half full? Yes, it can. Using the protective strategies discussed in this text you will learn how to profit from growth stocks in an expanding market while at the same time limiting the potential loss of capital from an unforeseen drop in the price of the stock.

The two protective strategies detailed in this text, married puts and collar trades, are covered positions. The investor will purchase shares of stock in 100 share blocks. For a married put trade, the investor will then purchase an equivalent number of put contracts to protect the underlying shares. In a collar spread, the investor will purchase shares of stock, purchase a put to protect the shares and at the same time sell an equivalent number of call contracts against the shares. Although these are common option investing strategies, some of the more conservative married put techniques presented in this text are a little different from the conventional methods and were inspired by a colleague, Kurt Frankenberg of RadioActive Trading.

When an investor buys a put option, they have purchased the right to sell the shares of stock at the strike price. The put option acts as insurance for the underlying security. The stock could drop to $0.00 in value, but the put owner can still sell the shares of stock for the value of the put strike price. Let's find out more.

Chapter 1

STRATEGY INTRODUCTION AND COMPARISON

The two strategies discussed in this text, married puts and collar spreads, are considered protective strategies. Both methods allow investors to protect their investments and preserve account capital by using options to minimize the risk of simply owning shares of stock. Before we introduce the strategies, let's review the standard definitions of an option. If you are just starting to trade options, these concepts are essential. If you are already an intermediate or experienced options investor, you might be able to skim through this section.

OPTIONS DEFINED

Options are contracts that give investors the right, but not the obligation, to buy or sell shares of stock. Investors can trade these contracts just as they can buy or sell (short) shares of stock. Each option contract typically represents 100 shares of the underlying security. If an investor purchases one option contract they are purchasing the right to buy or sell 100 shares of the underlying security; five option contracts would represent 500 shares. There are two types of options used by investors: calls and puts.

Buying a call option gives the owner of the contract the right, but not the obligation, to *buy* shares of stock at a set price (called the strike price) at any time before the option expires (called the expiration date). Buying a put option gives the owner of the contract the right, but not the obligation, to *sell* (force someone to buy) shares of stock at a set strike price prior to the expiration date. These definitions apply to investors who purchase options speculating that the stock will rise or fall to make a profit. On the other side of these transactions are options sellers. Selling a call obligates the investor to deliver shares of stock at the strike price to the option buyer. Selling a put obligates the investor to buy shares of stock at the strike price.

Table 1.1: Option Rights / Obligation Chart

	Buyer	**Seller**
Call	Owns the right to buy shares of stock from the call seller.	Obligated to deliver shares of stock to the call buyer.
Put	Owns the right to sell shares of stock to the put seller.	Obligated to buy shares of stock from the put buyer.

But, what does that really mean? Let's break Table 1.1 down to a more basic view.

Table 1.2: Option Position / Market Sentiment

	Buyer	**Seller**
Call	Speculative Bullish (Long Call)	Neutral to Bearish (Naked Call)
Put	Speculative Bearish (Long Put)	Neutral to Bullish (Naked Put)

Table 1.1 showed the rights and obligations of an option buyer and option seller. Table 1.2 illustrates the market sentiment for the four basic option transactions. These four transactions are *uncovered positions*, meaning that no shares of the underlying stock are owned or shorted with the option trade.

The call buyer has purchased the right to buy shares of stock at a set price, called the *strike price*. This is a very bullish position, as the investor needs the stock to rise in price so the value of the call option will increase in value. The investor can then *exercise* the option and purchase shares of stock at the strike price, or simply *sell to close* the option to realize a profit. This is the long call position. Essentially the profit potential for a long call strategy is unlimited, as the stock could continue to rise indefinitely.

The put buyer has purchased the right to sell shares of stock at the strike price at any time between now and the *expiration date*. This is a very bearish position, as the investor needs the stock to fall in price so the put option will increase in value. The investor can then exercise the put option and force someone to buy shares of stock, or the investor can simply sell to close the option to realize a profit. This is the long put position.

The call seller has entered into a contract that obligates them to deliver shares of stock at the option strike price. The investor collects a premium when the option contract is sold. If the stock price remains below the strike price of the call, the option will *expire worthless* and the investor will keep the premium. This strategy is called a naked call trade and is a neutral to bearish position, as the investor hopes the stock remains at the same price or declines in value. This is a very risky strategy because the potential loss is unlimited. Theoretically, the stock price could rise infinitely. If there is a large increase in the stock price, the investor may be forced to buy shares of stock at the higher price to fulfill the obligation of the option contract. This could result in a significant loss. To avoid this, the call seller can *buy to close* the option contract at any time before expiration to limit the loss if the stock price goes against them.

The put seller has entered into a contract that obligates them to buy shares of stock at the option strike price. The investor will receive a premium in return for providing this obligation. If the stock price remains above the strike price, the put will expire worthless and the investor will keep the premium. This is the naked put trade, which is a neutral to bullish strategy and is used by investors to potentially buy shares of stock at a discount. The risk in this strategy is if the stock falls in price. The investor may be forced to buy shares of stock at the option strike price to cover the obligation, even though the stock is trading at a much lower price. However, the investor can buy to close the put obligation at any time prior to the expiration date to limit their losses if their sentiment on the position has changed.

We just introduced several concepts that you may or may not be familiar with, such as strike price, expiration date, premium, and the idea of an option expiring worthless. In order to fully understand how options work, you need to be sure you are very familiar with these concepts.

Strike Price

Each optionable stock will have several strike prices to choose from to buy or sell for both calls and puts (Figure 1.1). In the case of a call buyer, the strike price represents the price of the stock at which the call buyer has the right to purchase shares of stock from the call seller. If the stock price is trading above the strike price of the call, the option is in-the-money (ITM). The call buyer can exercise the call contract, buy shares of stock at the strike price, and then sell the shares at market for the higher value. The call seller would have to deliver shares of stock at the value of the strike price to fulfill the obligation, even though the market is offering a higher stock price. If the stock price is trading below the strike price of the call, the option is out-of-the-money (OTM). If the call option were OTM at expiration, the call would expire worthless. The call buyer would not exercise the right to buy shares of stock at the strike price when the stock could be purchased at a lower value.

Figure 1.1 – Option Chain - Stock XYZ trading at $50.00

	Strike	Call Sym		Put Sym	
Stock (XYZ) $50.00		Near Month Options - 30 days to expiration			
	35.00	XYZGG		XYZSG	Out of the Money Puts
	40.00	XYZGH	In the Money Calls	XYZSH	(Strike Price below
Option Strike	45.00	XYZGI	(highlighted)	XYZSI	Stock Price)
Prices	50.00	XYZGJ		XYZSJ	
	55.00	XYZGK	Out of the Money Calls	XYZSK	In the Money Puts
	60.00	XYZGL	(Strike price above	XYZSL	(highlighted)
	65.00	XYZGM	Stock Price)	XYZSM	

Source: PowerOptions (www.poweropt.com)

Put options have the opposite requirements of call options. A call buyer owns the right to purchase shares of stock, whereas a put buyer owns the right to sell shares of stock. A put buyer is a bearish investor, as the put will gain in value as the underlying security falls in price. For a put buyer, the strike price represents the value for which the investor can force the put seller to buy shares of stock. If the stock is trading below the put strike price, the put is in-the-money, the opposite from the call scenario. If the stock is trading below the put strike price, the put buyer can force the put seller to deliver shares of stock at a higher value than the current market price. If the stock is trading above the strike price, the put option is out-of-the-money and will expire worthless. The put buyer would not exercise the right to sell shares of stock at the strike price if the shares could be sold at the market for a higher value.

Table 1.3: ITM / OTM Quick Chart

	In-the-Money	Out-of-the-Money
Call	Stock Price above the Strike Price	Stock Price below the Strike Price
Put	Stock Price below the Strike Price	Stock Price above the Strike Price

Figure 1.2 – A Stock With MJSD Expiration Series

May 2008 16 days left	June 2008 51 days left	September 2008 142 days left	December 2008 233 days left
Call Strike-Symbol	Call Strike-Symbol	Call Strike-Symbol	Call Strike-Symbol
40.00 - HPEH	40.00 - HPFH	40.00 - HPIH	40.00 - HPLH
45.00 - HPEI	45.00 - HPFI	45.00 - HPII	45.00 - HPLI
50.00 - HPEJ	50.00 - HPFJ	50.00 - HPIJ	50.00 - HPLJ
55.00 - HPEK	55.00 - HPFK	55.00 - HPIK	55.00 - HPLK
60.00 - HPEL	60.00 - HPFL	60.00 - HPIL	60.00 - HPLL
65.00 - HPEM	65.00 - HPFM	65.00 - HPIM	65.00 - HPLM

Source: PowerOptions (www.poweropt.com)

Expiration Date

The owner of the contract, whether it is a call or a put, has a set time frame to exercise this right before the option expires. This is known as the expiration date. Standard stock equity options expire on the third Friday of the specific expiration month. Technically, options expire on the third Saturday of the specific expiration month, but the last day investors can actively trade, close, exercise, or assign their options is the third Friday. Some index options may expire on the morning of the third Friday or the third Thursday afternoon. Recently, some indexes have released weekly options and some ETFs (Exchange Traded Funds) have released quarterly expiration options. This text focuses on the standard expiration, those options that expire on the third Friday of every month.

Each optionable stock will have various expiration months that the investor can choose to buy or sell. These different months are referred to as the option series for that stock. There are three possible expiration series for an optionable stock.

JAJO - January, April, July, and October
FMAN - February, May, August, and November
MJSD - March, June, September, and December

Regardless of the expiration series, every optionable stock will have the near month available. The example in Figure 1.2 shows the MJSD series, but since the March and April expiration dates have already passed, May is listed as the near option. You can see that the July and August options are not available yet, but the options with those expiration dates will be released once the next expiration date passes.

The July options for this stock will be released the Monday following May expiration.

At the time of publication, 40% of the more than 3,000 optionable stocks, indexes, and ETFs also have LEAPS options available. LEAPS are Long-term Equity Anticipation Positions that typically have a January expiration date one or two years out in time. Some indexes and ETFs will have December or March expiration dates one or two years out in time. During the months of May through July, the near term January LEAPS shift to regular contracts and a new series of LEAPS one year further out in time will generally be released.

Recently, the conversion schedule for LEAPS has been adjusted. The near term January options still convert to regular options in the months of May, June, and July, but the new far out LEAPS are not scheduled to be released until September, October, and November. The conversion and release dates are determined by the option's expiration series. For example, those optionable stocks with LEAPS available in the January class (JAJO series) will have the near LEAPS options convert in May and the new two year out LEAPS will be available to trade in September. Those optionable stocks with LEAPS available in the February class (FMAN series) will have the near LEAPS convert in June and the new two year out LEAPS will be available to trade in October. For the March class (MJSD series) the near LEAPS will convert in July and the new two year out LEAPS will be available to trade in November.

LEAPS options are the same as near term options with the exceptions that the expiration date is further out in time and the option root symbol for a LEAPS option will be slightly different from the near term options.

Option Symbols

On the exchange, stocks, indexes, and ETFs are identified by a specific symbol. The same is true for options. Each option has its own specific symbol that identifies which underlying security the option is related to, the expiration month, the strike price for the option, and whether the option is a call or a put.

Referring back to Figure 1.2, we see that all of the options that are listed have the same first two letters: HP. The first two or three letters of an option symbol are the root letters and they identify the underlying security for the option. These particular options are for Helmerich & Payne, Inc., which trades under the symbol HP. Options for IBM, International Business Machines, have the root symbol IBM.

The next letter following the root letters of an option signifies the expiration month. In Figure 1.2, note that the third letter for each of the May call options is E, for June the third letter is F, and for September the third letter is I. For IBM, the May symbols would start off as IBME..., for June IBMF..., and for September IBMI.... The expiration month letter is always the second to last letter of the option symbol. Call options use the expiration month letters of A through L. Put options use the expiration month letters of M through Z. Table 1.4 is a quick reference chart for the expiration codes for every month for call and put options.

Table 1.4: Expiration Month Codes

	Jan	Feb	Mar	Apr	May	Jun	Jul	Aug	Sep	Oct	Nov	Dec
Calls	A	B	C	D	E	F	G	H	I	J	K	L
Puts	M	N	O	P	Q	R	S	T	U	V	W	X

The final letter of the option symbol designates the strike price of the option. In Figure 1.2 notice how all of the 55 strike call options end in the letter K and all of the 50 strike call options end in the letter J. The symbol for the 55 strike put for HP would also end in the letter K, just as the symbol for the 50 strike put would end in the letter J. Since there are so many different strikes on stocks of various prices, these numbers might also indicate other strikes as well. A 150 strike option will also end in J, as typically so will a 250 strike call and a 350 strike call.

You will not need to memorize these codes in order to be a successful options trader, but having the information close by or in the back of your mind might help you avoid any mistakes when placing a trade.

TRADING OPTIONS

Like shares of stock, option contracts are listed on the exchanges with a bid and an ask price. An option buyer will pay the value of the listed ask price where an option seller will collect a premium at the bid price. The market maker for the underlying security determines the bid and ask prices for each option. The difference between the bid price and the ask price is referred to as the bid-ask spread. The market maker can manipulate the market by setting the bid-ask spread wider apart. He earns money by purchasing contracts at the bid price and then selling them to the public at the ask price.

The bid-ask spread also prevents investors from buying large amounts of contracts and then selling them quickly, as this would cause an immediate loss on the position. Without the spread in place, it is possible that investors could manipulate volume by buying large amounts of contracts and then selling them right away without penalty.

Figure 1.3 – Stock XYZ at $50.00, 30 days to expiration

More Info	Strike	Call Sym	Opt Bid	Opt Ask	Put Sym	Opt Bid	Opt Ask
Stock (XYZ) $50.00				Near Month Options - 30 days to expiration			
▶	35.00	XYZGG	14.70	15.10	XYZSG	0.00	0.10
▶	40.00	XYZGH	9.70	10.50	XYZSH	0.00	0.15
▶	45.00	XYZGI	5.10	Bid - Ask Spread: 5.40	XYZSI	0.25	Bid-Ask Spread: 0.40
▶	50.00	XYZGJ	1.55	1.80	XYZSJ	1.65	1.85
▶	55.00	XYZGK	0.15	0.30	XYZSK	5.20	5.50
▶	60.00	XYZGL	0.00	0.10	XYZSL	9.80	10.40
▶	65.00	XYZGM	0.00	0.10		14.90	15.40

Source: PowerOptions (www.poweropt.com)

Figure 1.3 shows the bid-ask spread for calls and puts on a given stock. For the 50 strike call, the bid price is $1.55 and the ask price is $1.80. This spread makes it impractical for any investor or group of investors to buy a large number of contracts at the ask price and then sell them immediately because they would incur a $0.25 loss.

The bid-ask spread for the 50 strike put is slightly lower at $0.20; the bid price is $1.65 and the ask price is $1.85.

Since each contract represents 100 shares of the underlying security, the total cost to buy an option would be:

Option Ask Price * Number of Contracts * 100

In the above example, the ask price for the 50 strike call is $1.80. One contract would cost the option buyer $180 (plus commissions):

Option Ask Price * Number of Contracts * 100
$1.80 * 1 * 100 = $180 (plus commissions)

The investor pays $1.80 for each share that is represented by the contract. If an investor purchased 5 contracts, it would cost them $900; 10 contracts would cost the option investor $1,800.

For the 50 strike put the ask price is $1.85. An investor buying one contract would pay $185 (plus commissions), 5 contracts would cost $925, and 10 contracts would cost $1,850 (plus commissions).

Option Pricing Components

The option premium has two components, intrinsic value and time value.

Intrinsic value refers to the amount of monetary value the strike price of the option is in-the-money (ITM). As noted earlier, a call option is ITM if the stock price is trading above the strike price. For an ITM call:

Intrinsic Value = Current Stock Price – Strike Price

(if the stock price is greater than the call strike price).

The put option is ITM if the stock price is below the strike price of the option. For an ITM put:

Intrinsic Value = Strike Price – Stock Price

(if the stock price is less than the put strike price).

Figure 1.3 shows that the 45 call has an ask price of $5.40. If XYZ is trading at $50.00, the 45 strike option is 5 points ITM, or has $5.00 of intrinsic value. Remember, a call buyer is purchasing a contract that gives them the right to buy shares of stock at the value of the strike price. Since the 45 strike call is below the current stock price, the option seller must collect at least the intrinsic value of the option in order for the trade to be practical.

Why would the option seller agree to give up their shares of stock for less than the current market value? If the option seller could only receive $3.00 to give another investor the right to buy their shares of stock for $4.00 less then the market price, no one would trade options. This is why the option premium must at least equal the intrinsic value of the option strike price.

The same philosophies apply to the put option. In Figure 1.3, the 55 strike put has an ask price of $5.50. Since XYZ is trading at $50.00, the 55 strike put is 5 points ITM, or has $5.00 of intrinsic value. A put buyer is purchasing the right to sell shares of stock at the value of the strike price. The put seller, who is obligated to buy the shares of stock, must collect at least the intrinsic value for the trade to be fair.

Why would the put seller agree to buy shares of stock for a higher price than the current market value if he did not receive adequate compensation?

Out-of-the-money (OTM) options do not have intrinsic value. The premium for OTM options is comprised completely of time value.

Time value refers to the dollar amount the option buyer is paying for the time until the expiration date and the option seller is collecting for the time to expiration.

In our example:

Stock XYZ is trading at $50.00.
The 45 call has an ask price of $5.40.
The 45 call is 5 points ITM. ($50.00 – $45.00).
The remaining $0.40 is the time value for that option.

The $0.40 represents the premium the call buyer pays for the right to buy shares of stock any time during the next 30 days. This means that the call buyer is paying slightly more than $0.01 per day for the right to buy the shares of XYZ at $45.00 per share.

$0.40 time value / 30 days remaining to expiration
= $0.0133 per day

For the 55 strike put:
Stock XYZ is trading at $50.00.
The 55 put has an ask price of $5.50.
The 55 put is 5 points ITM ($55.00 - $50.00).
The remaining $0.50 is the time value for that option.

The $0.50 represents the premium the put buyer will pay for the right to sell shares of stock during the next 30 days. Here we see that the put buyer is paying almost $0.02 per day for this right.

$0.50 time value / 30 days remaining to expiration = $0.0166 per day

For OTM options, the listed price is the time value for that option. In Figure 1.3 the ask price for the 55 strike call is $0.30. Remember, the 55 call is OTM because the stock is currently trading below the strike price. The 55 call has no intrinsic value. An investor who purchases the 55 call is speculating on a sudden rise in the stock to make a profit. If XYZ were still trading at $50.00 at expiration, the 55 call option would expire worthless. The call buyer would not exercise the right to purchase shares of stock at $55 when shares could be purchased directly on the market for less. If the call option expires worthless, the long call speculator would lose the full amount of the call purchase price.

In Figure 1.3 the ask price for the OTM 45 put is $0.40. The put is OTM because the stock price is trading above the put strike price. An investor who purchased the 45 put is speculating that the stock will drop in price. If XYZ falls below $45, the put buyer can force the put seller to deliver shares of stock for a higher value than the market price. If XYZ remains at $50.00 or rises, the 45 put will expire worthless. The put buyer would not exercise the right to sell shares of stock at 45 when the shares could be sold at the market price for a higher value.

PUTTING CONCEPTS TOGETHER

Earlier in this chapter, the option series for optionable stocks were discussed. The concepts of time value were just discussed.

Question: If an investor buys or sells an option with a further out expiration date, do they have to pay or collect more for that option?

Answer: Yes. Options that are bought or sold further out in time will have a higher time value for the same strike price.

As expiration day approaches, the time value on all options will decay. At expiration, any ITM options, whether they are calls or puts, will only retain their intrinsic value and all OTM options will expire worthless because they no longer have any inherent value.

Figure 1.4 shows the XYZ chain again, this time with the time value and percent (%) time value (the time value amount represented as a percentage of the underlying stock price) amounts shown for different expiration months.

Figure 1.4 shows the time value for the near month 50 call (30 days left to expiration) is $1.55.

Figure 1.4 - Option Chain - Stock XYZ trading at $50.00

More Info	Strike	Opt Bid	Opt Ask	Time Value	% Time Value	Opt Bid	Opt Ask	Time Value	% Time Value
Stock (XYZ) $50.00				Near Month Options - 30 days to expiration					
	40.00	9.70	10.50	-0.08	-0.2%	0.00	0.15	-	-
	45.00	5.10	5.50	0.32	0.6%	0.25	0.40	0.25	0.5%
	50.00	1.55	1.80	1.55	3.1%	1.60	1.85	1.38	2.8%
	55.00	0.15	0.30	0.15	0.3%	5.10	5.50	-0.12	-0.2%
	60.00	0.00	0.10	-	-	9.80	10.40	-0.42	-0.8%
Stock (XYZ) $50.00				4 Month Out Options - 120 days to expiration					
	35.00	15.10	15.60	0.32	0.6%	0.10	0.25	0.10	0.2%
	40.00	10.40	11.10	0.62	1.2%	0.40	0.55	0.40	0.8%
	45.00	6.40	6.70	1.62	3.3%	1.20	1.40	1.20	2.4%
	50.00	3.10	3.50	3.10	6.2%	2.90	3.20	2.68	5.4%
	55.00	1.20	1.40	1.20	2.4%	5.90	6.30	0.68	1.4%
	60.00	0.30	0.50	0.30	0.6%	10.10	10.50	-0.12	-0.2%

Source: PowerOptions (www.poweropt.com)

The corresponding 4 month out 50 call (120 days left to expiration) has a time value of $3.10.

A call seller would collect an additional $1.55 of time value for 90 more days until the option reaches expiration. Time value is the fee collected by the writer and the added cost that is paid by the option buyer. Time value works for the option seller as the premium decays over time, meaning that time value works against an option buyer.

PUTTING CONCEPTS TOGETHER

Notice in Figure 1.4 that the at-the-money options, those closest to the stock price, have the highest time value in each month. The near month 50 strike call and 50 strike put have a time value of 3.1% and 2.8% respectively, the 4 month out 50 strike call and 50 strike put 6.2% and 5.4%. The ATM options will always have the highest time value for an optionable stock.

CASE STUDIES

Purchasing a put option against shares of stock acts as insurance for the position. The investor can now sell the stock at the put strike price at any time through expiration. Even if the stock dropped to $0.00, the investor can exercise the put, forcing someone to buy the shares at the put strike price. When an investor sells a call, they are obligated to deliver shares of stock at the strike price. If an investor sells a call without owning a stock it is called a naked call. The naked call strategy is a neutral to bearish strategy. When an investor sells a call against shares that they own it is called a covered call trade. Since the stock is owned, the investor benefits when the stock moves up. The covered call trade is a neutral to bullish strategy, as the investor now wants the stock to go up in price. However, in the covered call strategy, the investor is only protected by the amount of premium they receive when they sell the call. This may only be about 2 or 3% of the underlying share price. When an investor sells the call and purchases a put option, the premium received from the sale of the call will pay for or reduce the price of the put option. The investor has limited the maximum risk on the position by purchasing the put option, but has also generated income by selling the call. Using a simple example is the best way to compare these techniques.

Example Trade: Long Stock Position

You have come across a stock that you feel might gain in value over the next two or three months. You might have read analysts' reviews of the stock and felt that it was in a competitive sector, you might have heard the stock mentioned at the office or you might have heard the stock discussed at a dinner party with friends or relatives. You may have been tracking the stock for some time and were waiting for the stock to hit your target buy price.

Regardless of the situation, you have decided to purchase 100 shares of the underlying security.

Long Stock Position

Stock XYZ @ $50.00
Buy 100 shares of stock XYZ at $50.00 per share
Total Cost = $5,000 (# of shares * price per share)
Potential Profit: Unlimited
Maximum Risk = $5,000 (100% of the investment amount)

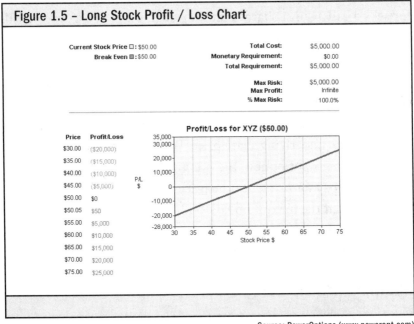

Figure 1.5 – Long Stock Profit / Loss Chart

Current Stock Price ☐: $50.00	
Break Even ■: $50.00	

Total Cost:	$5,000.00
Monetary Requirement:	$0.00
Total Requirement:	$5,000.00
Max Risk:	$5,000.00
Max Profit:	Infinite
% Max Risk:	100.0%

Price	Profit/Loss
$30.00	($20,000)
$35.00	($15,000)
$40.00	($10,000)
$45.00	($5,000)
$50.00	$0
$50.05	$50
$55.00	$5,000
$60.00	$10,000
$65.00	$15,000
$70.00	$20,000
$75.00	$25,000

Source: PowerOptions (www.poweropt.com)

When you purchase shares of stock you are investing in the company. You need the stock to increase in value in order to make a profit. Bare minimum, the investor wants the stock to remain at the purchase price over time so they don't see red in their portfolio and have to contemplate closing the position for a loss. Worst case scenario, the stock plummets in value due to some unforeseen event and you are left holding on to shares that are trading at 25 percent, 50 percent, or more below the initial purchase price. You have unlimited time for the stock to move in the desired direction, but that also means the position is vulnerable to fluctuations, specifically declines, over time.

Of course, there are ways that you can protect the stock position through a broker. With ever-increasing computer and internet technology and the advances of electronic exchange trading, it has become easier for investors to instantly place stop orders on stock positions. When an order to buy shares of stock is placed, you can instantly place various stop orders with a broker to limit the potential loss on the stock position.

If you had placed the trade as outlined in this example, you could immediately place a stop loss order or a trailing stop once the order was filled. Many brokers will allow investors to enter stop loss orders when the initial buy order is being placed.

However, these stop loss orders have drawbacks that can cause fits for investors. Stop loss orders do not protect against after-hours or pre-market moves. Earnings releases, early earnings warnings that happen after hours or over the weekend, reports of incorrect earnings statements, potential scandals, or scrupulous activity can all cause a significant decline in the price of the stock when the market is not open.

You may have decided to limit the losses to 8 percent of the underlying stock price, which is a common practice of many investors. Once the trade was entered a stop order could have been placed at $46.00

($4.00 is 8% of $50.00). The broker would automatically sell to close the position if the underlying shares dropped to $46.00 during the trading day.

Even though the position was thoroughly researched and the indicators signaled this was a bullish stock, the company might still have one of the aforementioned negative events during the after-hours or pre-market periods. The stock could be trading at $51.00 at Friday's close, but if negative news came out over the weekend, the stock could be trading well below the $46.00 stop point on Monday at market open. If the stock opened at $39.00 (a 24% drop in the stock's value from the previous close), the broker would not have been able to close the stock at $46.00.

You would then be facing a 24 percent unrealized loss on the position. You could sell to close the shares and take the loss, or hold on to the position hoping that the stock would rise in price at a later date. However, the position may not come back up to a reasonable price for several months and you may be left holding the shares for an extended period of time before it rebounds.

These after-hours or pre-market events are relatively uncommon but they do happen, usually at times when they are the least expected. If you have traded stocks before, you probably have at least one memory or black mark in your portfolio from such an event, or you most likely have heard tales of woe and loss from other investors in the marketplace. There are numerous examples of these events, ranging from risky bio-tech stocks where the FDA gives a failing judgment on a Phase II or Phase III drug trial; volatile stocks where investors are heavily speculating on an upcoming earnings event that fails to meet the analysts' target; companies that get caught misleading investors or announcements of a potential bankruptcy or extreme loss of revenue due to unforeseen economic events. The names Enron and Bear Stearns come to mind as extreme examples of these kinds of events that took investors by surprise.

So, the question begs to be asked: How can an investor better protect the long stock position during market hours, while at the same time protect against cataclysmic events that can happen when the market is closed?

Example Trade: Married Put Position

In order to protect the long stock position against all events, you could purchase a put option against those shares. This is called a Married Put strategy.

Recall that purchasing a put option gives the owner of the put the right to force someone to buy shares of stock at a set price, acting as insurance. The put option gives you the right to force someone to buy the long stock at the put strike price, regardless of how far the stock drops in value.

When you purchase shares of stock, you are making an investment in the company. The stock is an asset in your portfolio that you are expecting to increase in value over time.

When you make other large investments, don't you typically purchase insurance for those assets?

When you bought your house, you also bought home insurance to protect the investment and the valuables contained within that asset against the unforeseen: fire damage, theft and burglary, and perhaps you even bought extra insurance to protect against flood damage. If you own a car, you naturally have car insurance to protect the value of the vehicle against accidents, storm damage or any other unforeseen event. If you own any other luxury item such as a classic car, a boat or a valuable work of art, you most likely have those assets insured as well to protect their value as best you can.

If you purchase a large amount of stock, don't you want to insure that investment as well?

Standard Married Put Position
Buy 100 shares of stock XYZ at $50.00
Stock Purchase Cost = $5,000
Buy to Open 1 contract, 1 month out 45 strike put at $0.50
Total Put Cost = $50 (1 contract * 100 shares per contract * $0.50)
Total Position Cost = $5,050
Potential Profit: Unlimited
Maximum Risk = $550 (10.9 percent of the total investment)

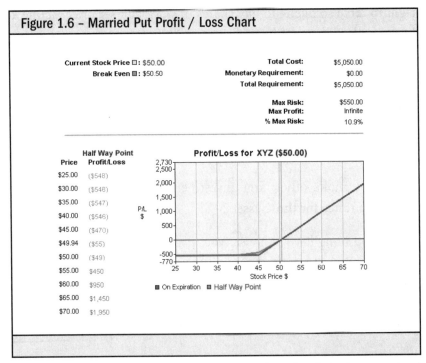

| | Figure 1.6 - Married Put Profit / Loss Chart |

Current Stock Price □: $50.00
Break Even ■: $50.50

Total Cost:	$5,050.00
Monetary Requirement:	$0.00
Total Requirement:	$5,050.00
Max Risk:	$550.00
Max Profit:	Infinite
% Max Risk:	10.9%

Half Way Point

Profit/Loss for XYZ ($50.00)

Price	Profit/Loss
$25.00	($548)
$30.00	($548)
$35.00	($547)
$40.00	($546)
$45.00	($470)
$49.94	($55)
$50.00	($49)
$55.00	$450
$60.00	$950
$65.00	$1,450
$70.00	$1,950

■ On Expiration ■ Half Way Point

Source: PowerOptions (www.poweropt.com)

In this example, the purchased put acts as insurance for the stock investment. The purchased put gives you the right to force someone to buy the shares of stock at the strike price, regardless of the trading price of the stock. Here, the 45 strike put has been purchased. Even if there was an early earnings warning announcement, an SEC investigation into falsely reported past earnings, or any other negative event occurred when the market was closed, the put can be exercised, forcing the put seller to buy the stock at $45.00, even if the stock had dropped to $5.00 in value.

It is important to note that in this example, the protective put cost only 1 percent of the investment to limit the maximum risk to only 11 percent of the total cost of the position! The put option protects the value of the stock in any situation, unlike insurance on a house or a car. If the value of your car declines because of age, your insurance policy will not cover that value. With home insurance, you will have different policies regarding damage to fire, theft or flooding. The insurance of the put option protects the stock value from any negative market situation.

The married put position still allows the investor to have potentially unlimited profits if the stock increases in value by a large amount. The total profit on the married put position will be slightly lower than owning shares of stock outright since purchasing the put option increased the total cost basis.

In the the long stock position example, the cost basis was equal to $50.00 per share. With the married put, the total cost basis is equal to the price of the underlying shares *plus* the cost of the put option. The underlying shares cost $50.00 per share and the put option cost $0.50 per contract. Remember, each contract typically represents 100 shares of the underlying security. Therefore, the cost for one contract would be $50.

$0.50 * 1 contract * 100 shares per contract

The total cost would be $5,050 and the effective cost basis would be $50.50 per share. If the stock were trading at any price above $50.50 at expiration, a profit would be realized.

The following tables show a simple breakdown between the long stock position and the married put position.

Table 1.5: Trade Comparison

Position	Cost of Position	Max. Risk	Max. Profit
Long 100 Shares XYZ @ $50.00	$5,000 (plus commission)	$5,000 (plus commission)	Unlimited
Married Put: Long 100 Shares + 45 Strike Put @ $50.50	$5,050 (plus commission)	$550 (plus commission)	Unlimited

Table 1.6: Position Value at Expiration

Stock Price at expiration	Long Stock Profit / Loss	Married Put Profit / Loss
$30.00	- ($2000.00)	- ($550.00)
$35.00	- ($1500.00)	- ($550.00)
$40.00	- ($1000.00)	- ($550.00)
$45.00	- ($500.00)	- ($550.00)
$50.00	$0.00	-($50.00)
$55.00	+ $500.00	+ $450.00
$60.00	+ $1000.00	+ $950.00
$65.00	+ $1500.00	+ $1450.00
$70.00	+ $2000.00	+ $1950.00

Table 1.6 illustrates that an investor trading the married put position would greatly reduce the maximum loss of the position while at the same time not sacrificing too much of the potential profit.

Example Trade: Collar Spread Position

One of the drawbacks of the standard married put position is that an extra premium is paid to enter the position. Many option investors prefer to sell options to generate income. Call or put options can be sold to generate income for a covered or uncovered position, depending on market sentiment and personal risk-reward tolerance.

In a standard collar spread strategy, shares of the underlying stock are purchased, a one month out, out-of-the-money put is purchased for protection, and an at-the-money or out-of-the-money call option is sold against the underlying shares.

The premium generated from selling the call option will cover the cost of the purchased put. Income, or a credit, is generated against the shares of the underlying stock while the benefit of protection, in the form of the purchased put, is still in place. Since income is generated, the overall cost basis for the position is lowered, as is the break even point and the maximum risk.

Collar Spread Position

Buy 100 shares of stock XYZ at $50.00
Stock Purchase Cost = $5,000
Buy to Open 1 contract, 1 month out 45 strike put at $0.50
Sell to Open 1 contract, 1 month out 55 strike call at $1.00
Total Option Premium (Credit) = -$0.50 (put premium − call premium)
($0.50 * 1 contract * 100 − ($1.00 * 1 contract * 100))
Total Position Cost = $4,950
Maximum Profit = $550
Maximum Risk = $450 (10.9 percent of the total investment)

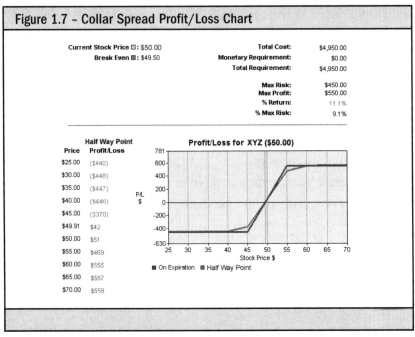

Figure 1.7 – Collar Spread Profit/Loss Chart

Current Stock Price □: $50.00
Break Even ■: $49.50

Total Cost:	$4,950.00
Monetary Requirement:	$0.00
Total Requirement:	$4,950.00
Max Risk:	$450.00
Max Profit:	$550.00
% Return:	11.1%
% Max Risk:	9.1%

Half Way Point

Profit/Loss for XYZ ($50.00)

Price	Profit/Loss
$25.00	($448)
$30.00	($448)
$35.00	($447)
$40.00	($446)
$45.00	($370)
$49.91	$42
$50.00	$51
$55.00	$469
$60.00	$555
$65.00	$557
$70.00	$558

■ On Expiration   ■ Half Way Point

Source: PowerOptions (www.poweropt.com)

The collar spread is still protected against a major decline in the share price due to any unforeseen event. The cost basis is lowered slightly due to the income that was generated from selling a call option against the underlying shares. In the married put example, the investor's cost basis was $50.50 per share. The cost basis included the price per share of the underlying security and the total premium paid for the put option to protect the shares.

By selling a call option and entering into a collar spread, the $1.00 premium generated from selling the call covers the cost of the put option while at the same time lowering the effective cost basis of the total position to $49.50. You still have the right to force the put seller to purchase the shares of stock at $45.00 in the case of a major decline in the stock price, thus the total risk on the position is only $4.50 per share. The maximum risk is lowered to 9.1 percent of the total capital invested.

Although the cost basis has been lowered and the collar spread offers slightly less maximum risk over the married put position in these examples, does that mean that the collar spread is a better strategy than a married put position? The answer is yes and no. The only way to answer that question correctly is to look into the future and see the closing price of the stock at the expiration date.

When a call option is sold against underlying shares of stock, there is an obligation to deliver shares of stock at the strike price. In the collar spread example, the 55 strike call was sold. If the stock rose to $60 per share, $70 per share or even $80 per share, the shares of stock would be sold at $55.00 to cover the obligation. The maximum profit would be only $550, but this is still an 11.1 percent return for a 30-day period.

REVIEW

The following tables show a simple breakdown between the long stock position, the married put position, and the collar spread position.

Tables 1.7 and 1.8 show the profit and loss advantages of a long stock position, the married put position, and the collar spread position. By looking at the profit and loss graphs of each position (figure 1.5, figure 1.6, and figure 1.7, respectively) and reviewing the monetary profit and loss values from the tables, we can easily see that the best position to trade is based on our expectation of the underlying security.

Table 1.7: Trade Comparison

Position	Cost of Position	Max. Risk	Max. Profit
Long 100 Shares XYZ @ $50.00	$5,000 (plus commission)	$5,000 (plus commission)	Unlimited
Married Put: Long 100 Shares + 45 Strike Put @ $50.50	$5,050 (plus commission)	$550 (plus commission)	Unlimited
Collar Spread: Long 100 Shares + 45 Strike Put − 55 Strike Call @ $49.50	$4,950 (plus commission)	$450 (plus commission)	$550 (plus commission)

Table 1.8: Position Value at Expiration

Stock Price at expiration	Long Stock Profit/Loss	Married Put Profit/Loss	Collar Spread Profit/Loss
$30.00	-(2000.00)	-($550.00)	-($450.00)
$35.00	-(1500.00)	-($550.00)	-($450.00)
$40.00	-(1000.00)	-($550.00)	-($450.00)
$45.00	-($500.00)	-($550.00)	-($450.00)
$50.00	$0.00	-($50.00)	+ $50.00
$55.00	+ $500.00	+ $450.00	+ $550.00
$60.00	+$1000.00	+ $950.00	+ $550.00
$65.00	+$1500.00	+$1450.00	+ $550.00
$70.00	+$2000.00	+$1950.00	+ $550.00

A long stock position would yield the highest potential return if the stock moved up in price, but the position is not protected from any unforeseen events or major market declines.

The married put position protects the underlying shares of stock against any major declines. This means that even in the worst unforeseen events only a limited loss would be realized. Most of the capital in the account would be preserved and could be reinvested into another position.

The collar position generates income by adding a sold call to the married put position. The premium received for selling the call should cover the cost of the put option that was purchased as insurance. The collar position limits the maximum profit that can be achieved since the return is capped by the obligation of the sold call. The collar position may yield a two or three percent return in a given month if the call is assigned at expiration. The collar position is also protected against any major declines with the put option in place.

The examples shown in this chapter show how a standard married put or standard collar position can limit losses compared to simply holding the stock. There are dozens of options strategies an investor can use to generate income or speculate on a bullish stock. In the next chapter we will further illustrate why you should use these two protective strategies in your portfolio and the advantages of these positions over some commonly used options trading strategies.

Chapter 2

THEORY BEHIND THE PROTECTIVE STRATEGIES

WHY USE PROTECTIVE STRATEGIES?

Over the years, the co-authors of this book have assisted many stock and options investors with strategy discussion, management techniques and general options education. We learn something new every day regarding the various techniques and approaches to options strategies, from the simple covered call trade to complex multi-legged strategies.

One thing remaining constant over the years is the overwhelming investor aversion to protective strategies. Many investors will see the benefit of protective strategies once they experience a losing position or after something drastic happens which they could never have ascertained through chart patterns, trend lines, or fundamental analysis. The basic principle of these protective strategies is investors needing to purchase an option to act as insurance for the underlying securities in their portfolio. It is our sentiment that many investors feel this basic principle is counter intuitive to the general philosophy of investing.

An investor purchasing shares of stock is looking for the stock to increase in price so the shares can be sold at a higher price to realize a profit. The investor may be looking for a short-term gain on a quick moving stock or may be looking for a long-term growth investment as retirement approaches. An investor may spend countless hours analyzing stock charts and fundamental data, comparing industry reviews or stock performance within the same sector or industry and may even use more elaborate techniques such as candlestick chart patterns or Fibonacci trends. Based on this analysis, an investor might select a target price for the stock at what he considers to be the best purchase price and a target price to exit the position.

Does this mean that the selected stock is guaranteed to move up in price over the next month, six months, or twelve months because the stock fits the selected criteria? Of course not. The market moves in trends and cycles and a stock selection method that worked well last year or even six months ago may not apply to current market conditions.

After an investor has put a significant amount of time into researching securities to purchase, is he prepared or even willing to admit the stock might decline in value? Most likely the answer is "no." An investor may prepare for declines in the stock by setting stop losses or trailing stops with a broker; alternatively, a mental stop might be used to plan on closing the position. The thought of purchasing an option for protective purposes is almost insulting to some investors.

An investor purchasing a protective put option may consider the purchase to be an admission that his research and analysis may be incorrect. Many investors suffer from the human element or emotional factor of investing, as they do not like to be wrong and basic human nature makes it difficult to admit that they were wrong. An investor considering a stock selection that could possibly fall in price would never have entered the trade in the first place, right?

Another way to observe the human element or emotional factor is to consider this question: have you had a 100% success rate in the stocks that you have purchased over the last year, two years, or five years? If you have been 100% successful in every stock trade you have made, closing out the position at your desired profit level in your desired time frame, then you are probably not reading this book, but instead are most likely sitting on a beach somewhere, researching your next successful stock purchases with a laptop on one side of your chair and a margarita on the other.

One of our favorite phrases used by stock analysts and investment services making stock or security recommendations is, "We were not wrong, we were simply early." This common phrase is often used after a stock selection falls in price in the first 30 or 60 days. In a year or two the stock price might encounter the target price that was anticipated. Meanwhile, an investor is left holding a substantial stock position in the portfolio that has declined in value. The stock may move up in price in the next 6, 12, or 24 months where it can be sold for a profit, but it may not. The stock could also continue to fall in price, causing further unrealized losses in the portfolio. In reality, the recommendation for the stock to go up was not wrong, but as the pundits say, "it was just early."

Again, this illustrates the risk of the human element or emotional factor after an investor enters a position. Some investors may enter a stock position with a stop order in place with their broker or with a mental stop in the back of their minds. If the investor had placed a stop order or a trailing stop with their broker, the position would have been exited automatically. The investor would realize the loss he was willing to take on the initial position and he could then take the remaining funds and invest in a new position that would hopefully make a profit. Quite often after an investor is stopped out of a stock and takes the realized loss, he will grow increasingly aggravated as the stock recovers in price. After a week or two, the stock might return to his initial purchase price.

A negative experience with a stop loss can also lead many investors to feel slightly paranoid in addition to being very frustrated. An investor may feel that someone is out to get his shares by purposely forcing the stock to drop in price and then forcing it back up in price. However, there are no "market gremlins" hidden in the exchange computers looking for stop orders, and market makers are not standing behind their screens laughing when a stop order is placed. When a stock position is entered, most likely the investor checked the average daily volume or the market capitalization. His minimum requirement may be that the stock trades an average daily volume of at least 500,000 shares per day and has a market capitalization of at least two billion (mid cap or higher). With so much volume and activity, it is very unlikely that a market maker or non-existent gremlin would focus on 100, 500, or 1,000 shares of stock that had been purchased.

After a mental stop is hit, an investor has two choices: sell to close the stock and realize the initial loss set by the mental stop or reconsider the stop point. The investor may decide the recent decline in the stock price was an overreaction to a recent news event, or the investor may consider that the decline was simply a result of market conditions and that the stock may rebound in the next month or two.

Does this scenario seem familiar? How many stock positions have you entered after careful due diligence and analysis only to have the stock move in the opposite direction that you anticipated? You do not have to answer these questions of course, but many of you may be nodding your heads in agreement, or regretting the one or two stocks "that got away."

You are not alone. The co-authors of this book are also guilty of rethinking their initial mental stop points, as are many other investors just like you. Both authors have purchased shares of a particular stock at one time or another, watched the stock fall in value, and held on to the shares as the stock continued to decline, resolving that the stock had to come back up in price sooner or later. After all, how could all of our research and analysis possibly be wrong?

Trading Exercise: Confidence Builder

The next time you are stopped out of a stock for a small loss only to observe it recover after your position was closed, analyze the position and determine what went wrong. After you have performed the analysis, turn it into a positive: tell your friends or relatives, "If you ever want to know a great entry price for a given stock, just let me know. I'll tell you where I would set my stop, and that will be your entry point. I can almost guarantee that will be the low price and the stock will rebound after it hits that level."

POTENTIAL UNFORESEEN PROBLEMS WITH LONG STOCK POSITIONS

So, the main reason to consider using protective strategies is to limit your risk of loss due to the following potential problems that might occur with a long stock position.

1. Incorrect timing ("We were not wrong, we were early")
2. Weakness in the economy

3. Weakness in a particular sector or industry

4. Catastrophic events (such as 9/11) or geopolitical events

5. Less than expected earnings reports

6. Incorrect or falsified earnings reports (rare)

7. Early earnings warning announcements

8. Board room scandal

9. Patent lawsuits against the company

10. FDA approvals for bio-tech or pharmaceutical companies

Any one of these events listed above can cause a significant or substantial loss in a long stock position. Many of these events may occur in the after-market or pre-market hours, causing a large decrease in the stock price when the trading floor is closed. This means your stop order or trailing stop will not be triggered and you will have to rush to place a sell order at a much lower price than your selected stop or you will be left holding the position for an unrealized loss.

COMMON MANAGEMENT TECHNIQUES

After one of these events occurs and your position has dropped in value, you probably have a list of management techniques that you would apply to the position. Let's take a look at some of the drawbacks of the more common long stock management techniques.

Common Technique #1: Don't sell the position for a loss, it will come back up.

Problems with Technique #1: Will it? This all depends on the type of event that caused the significant decline and the new market sentiment for the stock after the event. How long can you leave your capital tied up in a declining stock, or a stock that has fallen significantly but now is simply stagnating in price? How many other stocks are available for you to invest in?

Common Technique #2: Sell the position for the loss and reinvest.

Problems with Technique #2: Although this approach might protect you from further losses on the initial stock, what happens if the stock in which you reinvest also falls in price? How many losses can you take over a quarter, 6 month period, or 12 month period before your available investment funds are wiped out?

Common Technique #3: Buy more shares at the lower price and average down.

Problems with Technique #3: Danger! Danger, Will Robinson! You purchased shares of XYZ at $50.00, an unforeseen event occurred and the stock is now trading at $30.00. You purchase an equal amount of shares at $30.00 so your total cost basis is now only $40.00. Whew, that's a relief, isn't it? You have turned an initial 40% loss into a 25% loss on a stock that is still declining in value. This technique will only work if the stock turns around and starts to come back up in price. If it stagnates or continues down, all you have done is entered more available capital into a losing position.

Common Technique #4: I can withstand a loss on one stock; I am heavily diversified.

Problems with Technique #4: If you are diversified, good for you. In fact, we would assume that most of you reading this book are diversified in one way or the other, as you should be. Diversifying a portfolio into a mix of stock positions, mutual funds, ETFs, bonds, or other investments is a common practice and one that we advocate. Being diversified will allow you to withstand single stock losses from most of the events listed above, but it will not protect against all unforeseen events. If the economy is weak as a whole, if there is a sell-off from an extended bubble, or if there is a catastrophic and unthinkable event, all stocks and mutual funds will be dragged down. Most funds invested in 401Ks and IRAs are invested in mutual funds, which are also at the mercy of the market. On the other end of the spectrum, being too diversified can reduce any large gains you might have on a single stock position, as it is only a small part of your entire portfolio.

Common Technique #5: Enter into a repair strategy using options against the stock.

Problems with Technique #5: What? The experts writing a book on options strategies are going to mention the problems of using options to repair a fallen stock? Yes, we are. There are correct ways to use options to repair a fallen stock, and there are incorrect ways to do so. Most options repair strategies only work if the stock recovers in price. Some of the potential repair strategies using options will lower your cost basis by a small amount, but can still result in having your position called away or assigned for a significant loss. Other repair strategies are so elaborate that you may be required to put up a substantial amount of additional capital, or what is referred to as margin, to place the repair trade. Again, this just means you have had to allocate more available funds into a losing position. We are not going to examine all of the potential options repair techniques that could be used but many will be discussed in comparison throughout this text.

HOW CAN PROTECTIVE STRATEGIES HELP?

Investors can establish married put positions or collar trades to greatly reduce their exposure and potential loss on long stock positions. These protective strategies can be entered so the investor is never at risk for more than 10 percent of their initial cost basis, even when an unforeseen negative event occurs. To recap some of the thoughts from Chapter 1, would you enter into a real estate investment without insuring the property? If you purchase a new car, wouldn't you also insure the vehicle? If you are looking to purchase shares of stock should you not also consider insuring that investment?

Even if you trade stocks with stop orders in place, you are not fully protected on the investment. A significant loss on the position will take a much larger percentage gain to get back to your initial starting basis. For example, let's say you invested $10,000 into a single long stock position. Even though you had a stop order in place, let's assume that one of the after-hours or pre-market unforeseen events occurred and you were finally able to get out of the position with a 30 percent loss, or a $3,000 loss from your initial $10,000 starting basis.

$10,000 initial starting basis * 30 percent = $3,000 loss
**$10,000 initial starting basis - $3,000 loss = $7,000 remaining
to invest**

You now have $7,000 remaining that you will reinvest into another position. You simply need the new stock position to rise 30 percent so you can get back to your initial starting basis, right? Wrong. Thirty percent of $7,000, your remaining amount that is invested, is only $2,100. Even if your next position rises 30 percent in value, your total portfolio value will only be $9,100.

$7,000 invested + $2,100 profit from a 30 percent
increase = $9,100

This means you are still 9 percent below your initial starting basis of $10,000.

$7,000 remaining invested * 30 percent gain = $2,100
$7,000 remaining invested + $2,100 gain = $9,100
$9,100 current value - $10,000 starting basis = -$900
(or a 9 percent loss from the initial starting basis)

In this scenario you would need a 43 percent gain on your second investment to recoup the 30 percent loss from the initial position.

$7,000 remaining invested * 43 percent gain = $3,010 profit
$7,000 remaining invested + $3,010 profit = $10,010 total value

This can also be seen in a diversified portfolio. In a $100,000 portfolio split evenly into various investment vehicles, one significant decline could still result in a substantial loss for the portfolio. If the portfolio was distributed evenly among mutual funds, ETFs, bonds, and a select group of stocks, the investor could withstand a significant decline without losing too much overall value but would need a larger percentage increase to get back to the initial starting basis.

For this portfolio, consider an investor placing $10,000 each into two mutual funds, investing $10,000 each into two different ETFs, investing $20,000 into bonds and investing $10,000 each into four stocks from different sectors or industries. We are not recommending this method for diversifying a portfolio, but we want to use this allocation to better outline the risks of not using protective strategies in a diversified portfolio.

$100,000 Starting Basis
$20,000 into 2 mutual funds ($10,000 into each mutual fund)
$20,000 into 2 ETFs ($10,000 into each ETF)
$20,000 into the bond market
$40,000 into 4 separate stock positions ($10,000 into each stock)

Over the course of a few months, you see that you have gained about one percent on the mutual funds, the two ETFs, and your investments in the bond market. Over that same time period, three of your stocks gained one percent as well, but you were stopped out for a 35 percent loss on the fourth stock position. Your portfolio value would be:

1 percent gain * $20,000 in mutual funds = $200
1 percent gain * $20,000 in ETFs = $200
1 percent gain * $20,000 in bond market = $200
1 percent gain * $30,000 in 3 stocks = $300
35 percent loss * $10,000 in 1 stock = -$3,500
Total Loss = $200 + $200 + $200 + $300 - $3,500 = -$2,600
Portfolio Value = $100,000 starting basis - $2,600 loss = $97,400

Because the portfolio was fairly diversified, the 35 percent loss on the one stock only dropped the portfolio by 2.6 percent of the initial starting basis ($2,600 loss from the initial starting basis of $100,000). However, it is extremely unlikely that the mutual fund positions, the ETF positions or the bond market value will increase by more than a few percent over the course of a month, quarter, or even six month period in an uncertain market. This means that the remainder of the 2.6 percent loss would have to be made up in the stock positions of the portfolio. The portfolio in this example gained $300 on three stock positions, but lost $3,500 on the fourth stock position. The remaining value to invest in the stock allocation of the portfolio would be:

$$\text{\$40,000 initial allocated funds + \$300 gain - \$3,500 loss =}$$
$$\text{\$36,800 total to invest}$$

If the investor kept the initial $30,000 invested in the three stocks that showed a slight gain, there would only be $6,800 remaining to invest in a new position. Regardless, the investor is still hoping that the $36,800 invested in the stock positions will soon recoup the initial $2,600 loss since the other positions typically only show returns of a few percent per year. This means that the investor would need to realize a 7 percent increase in the stock portion of the portfolio to make back the value lost on the fourth stock position.

$$\text{\$36,800 * 7 percent = \$2,576}$$

This would just about make up for the $2,600 total loss on the portfolio from the one stock position. However, in a down market, the mutual fund positions and ETF positions would also decline, adding to the loss in the portfolio value. The investor may need the stock positions to increase as much as ten percent each to counter the initial loss and any losses that might start piling up in the other positions of the portfolio allocation.

In Chapter 1 we showed how a simple married put position could limit the loss on a particular stock position to only ten percent, while only adding an extra one percent cost to the investor. Even in a diversified portfolio, a significant loss on only one position can greatly reduce the overall value and cause the investor to reallocate their funds and change their investing plan, or cause them to expect larger increases in certain positions that may be unrealistic.

These examples illustrate how protective strategies can help long stock investors or even diversified investors limit their initial losses even in the event of some catastrophic decline in a stock. We'll now consider how the married puts or collar spreads match up against some of the more common options investment strategies.

MARRIED PUTS AND COLLAR SPREADS VS. COMMON OPTIONS INVESTMENT STRATEGIES

The Long Call

Many new options investors are lured by the strategy of buying call options, what we call a *long call position.* When an investor purchases a call option they have the right, but not the obligation, to purchase shares of stock at a set price (the strike price of the purchased call option) at any time between now and the expiration date. Buying call

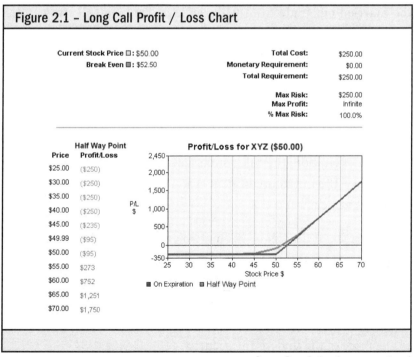

Figure 2.1 – Long Call Profit / Loss Chart

Current Stock Price □ : $50.00		Total Cost:	$250.00
Break Even ■ : $52.50		Monetary Requirement:	$0.00
		Total Requirement:	$250.00
		Max Risk:	$250.00
		Max Profit:	Infinite
		% Max Risk:	100.0%

Price	Half Way Point Profit/Loss
$25.00	($250)
$30.00	($250)
$35.00	($250)
$40.00	($250)
$45.00	($235)
$49.99	($95)
$50.00	($95)
$55.00	$273
$60.00	$752
$65.00	$1,251
$70.00	$1,750

Source: PowerOptions (www.poweropt.com)

options is a very bullish strategy. This strategy appeals to many new investors as they can potentially take advantage of an increase in the underlying stock but pay only a fraction of the cost of owning shares of the underlying stock.

Trading Example 2.1: Long Call Strategy

Stock XYZ trading at $50.00 per share
Buy to Open 1 contract, 1 month out 50 strike call at $2.50
Option Purchase Cost = $250.00 (1 contract * 100 shares per contract * $2.50)
Potential Profit: Unlimited
Maximum Risk = $250.00 (100 percent of the initial purchase price)

For those of you with a quick eye, you might have noticed that Figure 2.1 looks very similar to Figure 1.6, the profit/loss chart for the married put trade from Chapter 1. In the long call strategy the potential profits are unlimited, just like they are in a long stock position or in the married put position. The married put position and the long call positions are parity trades; each position has essentially the same risk-reward profile. As the stock gains in price, the call option will also gain in value. The maximum risk for the long call is equal to the cost of the position. If the stock falls in price and is trading below $50.00 at expiration, the call option will expire worthless. The investor will lose the initial investment amount, but cannot lose any more than that value, even if the stock drops to $0.00.

There is a slight difference in the two examples, however. The married put example from Chapter 1 illustrated purchasing the stock and at the same time purchasing an out-of-the-money 45 strike put option for $0.50. In this example, the one-month out long call position is at-the-money, meaning the strike price of the purchased option is equal to the price of the underlying security.

In this example, the investor would need the stock to be trading at $52.50 on expiration just to break even. The investor would need the stock to gain 5 percent over the 1 month expiration period in order to break even. If the stock is trading at $52.50 on expiration, the call option will have $2.50 of intrinsic value, since the investor purchased the 50 strike call option. The investor can exercise the call option and purchase 100 shares of stock at $50.00 or the investor could simply sell to close the call option for $2.50. If the stock is trading anywhere above the break even price of $52.50, the long call investor will realize a profit. For example, if the stock were trading at $55.00, at expiration the call option would have $5.00 of intrinsic value. The investor could sell to close the call option for $5.00, and realize a profit of $2.50 per contract, or 100 percent of the initial purchase price.

As exciting as this might sound, keep in mind the stock would have to gain 10 percent in a 1 month time frame in order for an investor to realize this 100 percent gain. This can happen in an extremely bullish market, but it is a fairly unrealistic expectation. The downside of this trade is that if the stock remains at the same price or falls slightly, the 50 strike call option will expire worthless. The investor in this example would lose the initial cost of $250. Although this seems like a small amount, it is a 100 percent loss on the position. Long call trading is a leveraged position, but leverage works both ways. The position can yield large returns if there is a significant movement in the stock price, but if the stock stagnates or declines in price, the investor can lose the entire amount they put into the position.

Think back to the married put example in Chapter 1. In that example the investor would have purchased 100 shares of XYZ at $50.00 and at the same time purchased a 1 month out 45 strike put option for $0.50. The total cost would have been $5,050, or $50.50 per share. If XYZ moved up one percent in 30 days, the married put position would be at break even. The long call investor needs a 5 percent gain to break even. If XYZ moved up 1 percent in 30 days, the long call investor could sell to close the option for $0.50. This would result in a $2.00 loss on a $2.50 investment, or an 80 percent loss on the position.

Trading Exercise: Historical Comparison

Take a look at the last five or ten stock purchases that you made. Using historical options data, go back and find the cost of the at-the-money call option on the date you entered the long stock trade, then compare the returns one month out in time. How did the long call trades stack up against the long stock positions?

(If you do not have access to historical options data, contact us at www. poweropt.com.)

In a long call position the investor does not own shares of the underlying security, they own a contract that gives them the right to buy shares of stock. The potential profits that can be realized in the long call position are based on the movement of the underlying stock. If the stock does not go up in price, the long call investor will lose money. Since the potential profits on the long call position are based on the stock moving up in price, the long call investor is still subject to the same problems as a long stock investor. Your broker may allow you to place stop orders or contingent orders on the long call position, where the position would automatically be closed if the stock hits a certain price or if the option premium drops. However, any unforeseen market events that would result in a gap down in the after-market or pre-market hours would not trigger the stop order and the long call investor would have a significant loss on the position. There are other common problems with long call investing.

1. **Over Trading.** Because call options cost a fraction of owning shares of stock outright, many investors will enter into too large of a long call position. If we had $5,000 to invest, we could purchase 100 shares of XYZ at $50.00, or we could purchase 20 contracts of the 50 strike calls at $2.50 a piece. These call contracts represent 2,000 shares of the underlying stock, or a total market value of $100,000 (2,000 shares * $50.00 current price)! This is extremely risky because all of the investor's available funds are placed into the long call position without any protection.

2. **Errant Diversification.** Because of the low cost of options, an investor may feel the need to purchase calls on a number of different stocks in an attempt to duplicate the diversification of a stock portfolio. Remember, the at-the-money long call position in the example above needed a 5 percent increase in the stock price simply to break even. A 10 percent increase in the long call example would have yielded a 100 percent return, or a profit of $2.50. What if an investor entered 10 long call positions with a similar cost and risk-reward profile as the example above? Even if 2 of the 10 stocks had a 10 percent increase, which would be a profit of about $5.00, what about the other 8 positions that also cost $2.50 to enter? The investor would need each of the 10 stocks to gain 5 percent in 1 month just to break even, or have several significant gains in order to balance out the total cost of all ten positions.

3. **Depreciating Assets.** Long calls are depreciating assets. Once an investor purchases an option speculating on a significant movement in the stock price, they are immediately fighting time. The investor in this example only has 30 days for the stock to gain in value to offset the cost of the option. If the stock stagnates and remains at $50.00 over the next month, the option will lose its entire premium of $2.50 over the expiration period.

Even if the stock rises in price, the option will still lose time value as each day passes.

4. **Speculating on Large Gains Costs More Premium.** You may know of a stock that has earnings coming up or you may have read about a stock that is expected to announce an extremely lucrative deal. You are not the only one in the marketplace that knows that earnings are coming up or that the stock has been in the news recently. There are many other investors that have heard the same information and are entering trades speculating that the stock will rise or fall within the next 30 days. This will cause the option premiums to be inflated as demand for the options increases. You will now have to pay more for each contract speculating on a change in the underlying security, still without any protection in place in case of any large movements against the position.

These common mistakes that are made by long call investors can lead to significant losses in the investor's portfolio. With the long call position, the investor is still at risk for the full amount of the investment even when stop orders are in place. If an unforeseen market event occurs, the long call can quickly lose 90 percent, 95 percent or 100 percent of the initial investment amount. In comparison, the maximum percentage losses of the married put and collar spread trade are drastically reduced. With the protective put in place, you are only at risk for a small percentage of the initial investment, even if the stock drops to $0.00 in value.

In addition, the collar spread allows the investor to generate income by selling a call option to help offset the cost of the protective put.

Trading Tip: Long Call Strategy

Most long call investors will not purchase the near term options that are less than 60 days to expiration. Typically, a long call investor will look to purchase the option that is several months out in time. This may cost a little more but it will give the investor more time for the stock to move in the desired direction to obtain a profit. Also, most long call investors would not hold the option to expiration but would sell to close the option during the expiration period if a reasonable profit was realized. We just wanted to use the basic example as a fair comparison. In the next chapter we will show you how using longer term puts in the married put strategy is more beneficial than using the near term, one-month out puts that were shown in the standard example from Chapter 1.

The Covered Call

For comparison, let's take a look at one of the most common income generating strategies used by options investors, the *covered call trade.*

Trading Example 2.2: Covered Call Strategy

Covered Call Position
Buy 100 shares of stock XYZ at $50.00
Stock Purchase Cost = $5,000
Sell to Open 1 contract, 1 month out 50 strike call at $2.25
Total Premium Collected = $225
(1 contract * 100 shares per contract * $2.25)
Total Position Cost = $4,775
Potential Profit: $225
Maximum Risk = $4,775 (4.5 percent less than the current trading
price of XYZ)

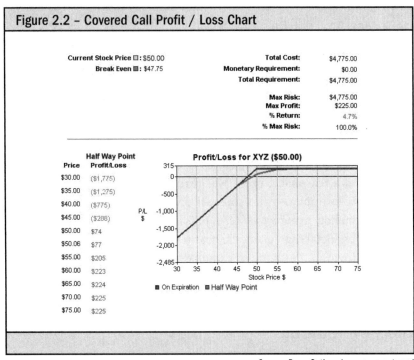

Figure 2.2 – Covered Call Profit / Loss Chart

Current Stock Price ☐: $50.00	Total Cost:	$4,775.00
Break Even ■: $47.75	Monetary Requirement:	$0.00
	Total Requirement:	$4,775.00
	Max Risk:	$4,775.00
	Max Profit:	$225.00
	% Return:	4.7%
	% Max Risk:	100.0%

Half Way Point

Price	Profit/Loss
$30.00	($1,775)
$35.00	($1,275)
$40.00	($775)
$45.00	($288)
$50.00	$74
$50.06	$77
$55.00	$205
$60.00	$223
$65.00	$224
$70.00	$225
$75.00	$225

Profit/Loss for XYZ ($50.00)

■ On Expiration ■ Half Way Point

Source: PowerOptions (www.poweropt.com)

In this strategy, an investor will sell a call option against the purchased shares of stock. By selling the call option the investor is obligated to deliver shares of stock at the strike price of the call if the stock is trading above that price at expiration. The investor collects a premium for selling the call option that helps protect the shares against a small drop. In this example, the stock can drop 4.5 percent (or $2.25 per share) before the investor is losing money on the transaction. Covered call trades are a neutral to bullish strategy as the investor is looking for the stock to stay at the same price or gain in value over the time between now and the expiration date. This example is an at-the-money covered call trade. To be more conservative, we might sell an in-the-money call option, which would give us slightly more protection, would lower our potential return if assigned, but would give us a higher probability of getting assigned and earning the return. At-the-money covered call positions have a roughly 50-50 probability of being assigned at expiration.

If the stock is above $50.00 at expiration, the investor will be assigned. This means that the investor will deliver the shares of stock for $50.00 per share and keep the $2.25 in premium from the sale of the call option, which is a 4.7 percent return compared to the total cost of the covered call position.

The covered call strategy is a conservative, income generating strategy and the co-authors of this book advocate trading this strategy over simply buying and holding shares of stock or speculating with long call or long put positions. Although we advocate covered calls as a conservative income generating strategy, there are some drawbacks.

First, in this strategy, the investor will have to buy shares of stock. Although a small premium is received from selling the call option that protects the purchased shares against a minor decline or a stagnating stock, there is no protection in place. The covered call investor could place stop orders on the covered call trade just as they could with the long stock position, but you are probably aware that there are some problems that can arise from placing stop orders. Also, if a stop is triggered between now and the expiration date, the covered call investor may also have to pay a small premium to buy to close the call option before the stock can be sold. If the call option is not closed before the shares of stock are sold, the investor is now in an uncovered naked call position, which is extremely risky.

Second, the covered call position limits the potential gains on the underlying stock position. If the stock rose 10 percent, 15 percent, or 20 percent over the expiration period, the investor would only realize the maximum 4.7 percent return. Although 4.7 percent is a fantastic monthly return, in our experience, you should not expect to make more than a 2.5 percent or 3 percent return when trading covered calls.

However, let's assume that you could place 10 at-the-money covered call trades that offered a 4.5 percent protection with about a 4.5 percent maximum return on each trade. The at-the-money covered call trades will have about a 50 percent probability of being assigned and earning the 4.5 percent return. At expiration, let's assume that five of our ten covered call trades were assigned and we earned 4.5 percent on each trade. The other five covered call trades were not assigned, so we can assume that we broke even for the month, correct?

Not necessarily. Even with stop orders in place, the other five covered call positions did not have the locked in protection that the married put trade or the collar spread trade would have given us. If one of the unforeseen events occur on one of the unassigned covered call trades, you may experience a significant loss. If five of the covered call positions were assigned, four of the remaining five positions declined to break even, but the last position suffered a 30 percent loss because of an unforeseen event, where would our portfolio stand? Assuming that we had allocated the same dollar amount into each position, we can simply add up the gains and losses.

Covered Call Returns

22.5 Percent (5 covered call positions with 4.5 percent return)
0 Percent (4 covered call positions that declined to break even)
<u>-30 Percent (1 covered call position declined 30 percent in value)</u>

Result: -7.5 Percent Loss (5 profitable covered calls, 4 break evens and 1 significant loss)

Sure, this may be an extreme example, but in an uncertain market this scenario is very likely when an investor is trading at-the-money covered calls. The unforeseen negative events that we have been discussing so much can happen at any time, regardless of the investor's research, analysis, and due diligence. Many naysayers of options strategies and advocates for speculative options investing strategies such as long calls will tell you that covered calls are a perfect strategy to filter out the winners in your portfolio from the losers: the winners will get called away for a limited return and the losers will pile up in your portfolio.

The co-authors of this book will agree with that statement, assuming that the investor simply enters the covered call trades but does not apply any proper management techniques when the stock moves up in price or declines in value. If an investor simply enters into a covered call trade hoping to get assigned and does not plan to manage the trade, that is exactly what can happen. Even though the investor collected some premium to protect the long stock position, without managing the position, they are essentially following the buy and hold method. They are hoping for an increase in the stock price so they will be assigned and earn the maximum return, but they are not prepared to roll the position if the stock falls in value. We hope that you do not fall into this category of investment methodology, but if you do, the protective married put strategy and collar spread trade will save your portfolio from many significant losses that you were not planning to manage.

Trading Tip: Covered Call Management Techniques

If you are trading covered calls but are unsure of the possible management techniques, you should visit the Learning Center on the PowerOptions web site and review the various Tip Sheets on covered call roll out techniques. You may also be interested in Ernie and Greg Zerenner's covered call course, *Covered Calls: Aggressive Strategy for the Conservative Investor*, which can be located on the PowerOptions web site (www.poweropt.com).

Bull Spreads as Parity Trades to Protective Strategies

Since we compared the standard long call position to its parity trade of the standard married put position, let's also take a look at the bull put credit spread and bull call debit spread strategy, which are parity trades to the standard collar spread.

The bull spreads are typically short-term positions that work best with neutral to bullish stocks. In a bull put credit spread, an investor will sell a slightly out-of-the-money put and then purchase a deeper out-of-the-money put for protection on the downside. The investor will receive a credit for this position because the premium received for the short (sold) put will be greater than the premium paid for the long put option. If the stock remains above the sold put strike price, both options will expire worthless and the investor will keep the net credit. The risk with this trade is if the stock falls below the break even point; the maximum loss is realized if the stock falls below the lower put strike price at expiration.

Trading Example 2.3: Bull Spreads
(Bull Put Credit and Bull Call Debit)

Bull Put Credit Spread
Stock XYZ trading at $50.00 per share
Sell to Open 1 contract, 1 month out 45 strike put for $0.75
Buy to Open 1 contract, 1 month out 50 strike put for $0.25
Total Net Credit = $0.50 (or $50.00; $0.50 credit * 1 contract
* 100 shares per contract)
Maximum Risk = $4.50 (Difference in Strike Prices – Net Credit)
Maximum Percent Return = 11.1 percent ($0.50 credit / $4.50 risk)

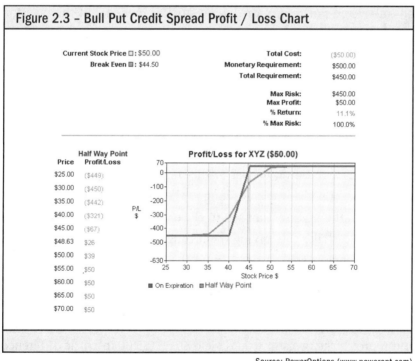

Figure 2.3 - Bull Put Credit Spread Profit / Loss Chart

Current Stock Price ☐: $50.00	Total Cost: ($50.00)
Break Even ■: $44.50	Monetary Requirement: $500.00
	Total Requirement: $450.00
	Max Risk: $450.00
	Max Profit: $50.00
	% Return: 11.1%
	% Max Risk: 100.0%

Profit/Loss for XYZ ($50.00)

Price	Half Way Point Profit/Loss
$25.00	($449)
$30.00	($450)
$35.00	($442)
$40.00	($321)
$45.00	($67)
$48.63	$26
$50.00	$39
$55.00	$50
$60.00	$50
$65.00	$50
$70.00	$50

■ On Expiration ■ Half Way Point

Source: PowerOptions (www.poweropt.com)

Again, an investor with a quick eye will notice that Figure 2.3 looks identical to Figure 1.7, the collar spread profit and loss chart. The slight difference is that the upper profit point is at the 45 strike price in this example since the out-of-the-money 45 strike put was sold. In the standard collar example from Chapter 1, the 55 strike call was sold, so the profit and loss chart was shifted more to the right. Both positions have a maximum risk of $450, but the standard collar example from Chapter 1 offered a higher maximum profit because the investor could take advantage of appreciation from the initial stock price to the sold call strike price. The bull put credit spread is an uncovered position, meaning no stock is owned, but the investor will still be required to have the maximum risk value on hold in their account to cover the position.

The bull call debit spread would have a very similar profit and loss chart as well. In the bull call debit spread the investor would sell the in-the-money 45 strike call and purchase the deeper in-the-money 40 strike call. The investor would pay a debit to enter the position since the purchased option is deeper in-the-money and would have a higher intrinsic value. However, as long as the stock stays above $45.00 at expiration, the investor can sell to close the 40 strike call and buy to close the 45 strike call, giving them roughly $5.00 of intrinsic value. The difference in strike prices minus the initial net debit is the maximum return for the debit spread position. In this example (though we will not show a chart for it), the initial net debit may have been around $4.50. If the position were closed at expiration for the maximum profit, the investor would yield $0.50 ($5.00 intrinsic difference - $4.50 initial debit).

We do not want to go into too many specifics of the bull spreads, but we did want to point out some of the risks of trading these positions.

Both bull spread positions offer a limited maximum loss just like the standard collar spread. The mistake that is commonly made with the bull spreads is that they are leveraged positions where no shares of the underlying stock are owned. If an investor has only $5,000 to invest, he could enter into a standard collar position as outlined in Chapter 1. The investor could buy 100 shares of XYZ, sell one 55 strike call and purchase one 45 strike put. The total amount invested in the collar position would be $4,950. Because the protective put has been purchased, the investor could not lose more than $450, or 9.1 percent of the initial amount invested.

Some of the problems with the bull spreads are similar to the problems shown with the long call example. The first potential mistake that investors might make when trading the bull spreads is overtrading. If the investor had the same $5,000 to invest and was interested in trading the bull put credit spread or the bull call debit spread, he may decide to trade 10 contracts instead of 1. The investor would not have to purchase shares of stock, but he would still be required to have the maximum risk on hold in his account for the credit spread or pay the total value for the debit spread. If 10 contracts were traded in either bull spread strategy, the maximum risk would now be $4,500. If the stock had a significant decline due to one of the unforeseen market events and the stock gapped down below the lower strike put or call, the investor would realize the maximum loss. This means the investor could stand to lose 90 percent of his initial $5,000 investment on one trade!

The errant diversification problem can also occur when trading bull put credit spreads or bull call debit spreads. Let's say that we had $5,000 to invest again and we selected 10 bull put credit spreads that had the same risk-reward profile of the spread outlined in Trading

Example 2.3. For each spread, the investor received a $0.50 net credit for a total of $500 in premium. Each spread requires $450 to be placed on hold in the account (the margin requirement) for a total of $4500.

You may be able to see the problem right away. The total income that was generated was $500. Each spread has a maximum risk of $450. Even with stop orders in place to limit the loss on the spread position, one negative unforeseen event can cause one of the spreads to hit the maximum loss in the after-market or pre-market hours. The stop order would not be able to be filled and that one loss would wipe out almost the entire month's profits. What if two out of the ten spread positions suffered a major decline caused by some unforeseen event? The investor would now have lost $900 on those two positions. This would wipe out the $500 in premiums generated this month and any profits that had been generated from the previous month as well. That's right, an 80 percent success rate for this month's trades wiped out all profits from the last two months. Again, this is just one of the problems with leveraged positions. The leverage works for you and can work against you as well.

Why Compare Only Long Calls and Covered Calls?

There are dozens of different options strategies that an investor can use to generate income, speculate on the rise or fall of a given security, or balance their portfolio. We wanted to focus on the long call and the covered call strategy for comparison for two specific reasons.

First, in order to trade options, an investor must typically apply with a broker to qualify for options tradeing. Even if you have never traded an option before, you might still be approved for Level 1 options trading. This will allow the investor to purchase call options or put options, and with most brokers, trade covered calls as well. This is all the approval you will need to trade married puts or collar spreads, but Level 1 approval will allow you to trade long calls and covered calls as well. We felt it was necessary to relate the pros and cons of these two strategies against the protective married put and collar spread strategies. We did not compare the long put strategy, as that is an aggressive bearish strategy, and married puts and collar spreads are protective bullish to neutral strategies.

Second, many investors will trade through IRAs or other retirement accounts. Most brokers will only allow the Level 1 strategies to be traded in these types of accounts. They will not allow the advanced options strategies such as credit spreads or debit spreads to be traded in retirement accounts.

Trading Tip: Protective Bearish Strategies

If you have a bearish sentiment on the market, the protective strategies discussed in this text may not apply to you, as they are protective strategies for a neutral to bullish market sentiment. However, many of the concepts that are discussed in this text can be applied to the bearish protective strategies: married calls and short collar positions. In a married call trade, the investor will short shares of stock and purchase a call option for protection; in a short collar the investor would short shares of stock, buy a call option for protection, and sell a put to generate income. You simply need to reverse the strategy discussion and apply the ideas to short positions for a bearish market.

REVIEW

There are many other options strategies used by investors to generate income or to speculate on movements in the underlying securities. We just wanted to focus on a few of the more common strategies to reflect how the protective strategies can greatly reduce your risk while at the same time put you in position to make a respectable profit. However, there are many different ways that an investor can approach trading the married put strategy or the collar spread strategy. An investor can adjust the position to be more conservative and have a very minimal risk in the near term, but they can also lower the potential risk even more by using protective put options that are further out in time, or deeper in the money.

In the next chapter we will discuss the various combinations that can be used in both protective strategies, the pros and cons of each potential combination, and when an investor might consider using one combination over another depending on their outlook of the underlying stock or their overall risk-reward tolerance.

Chapter 3

STRATEGIES WITHIN THE STRATEGIES

So far we have discussed the concepts behind the protective strategies and the ways you can benefit from these trades over simply trading long stocks or some of the other common options trading strategies. As the cliché goes, "options give you options." Each optionable stock will have several different expiration months that an investor can choose from when purchasing a put option or selling a call option to create a collar spread. The investor can also choose to purchase or sell in-the-money, at-the-money, or out-of-the-money options when constructing these protective strategies. The investor can choose a more conservative protective position if he is more interested in preserving capital, or an investor can decide to trade more aggressively while still only risking a small percentage of the position.

Each combination in either strategy has advantages and disadvantages that the investor needs to be aware of before placing a trade. Even though the basic collar trade is a neutral to bullish strategy, an investor can create a combination of buying stock, buying a put option, and selling a call option that will result in a bearish position.

Throughout this chapter we will look at the potential combinations for both strategies on the same fictitious stock. We will analyze the pros and cons of each combination and discuss when it may be best to use one particular combination over another. Although every stock is different, the comparisons in this chapter will provide you with a method to analyze the potential combinations and evaluate which technique might work best based on your sentiment of the underlying stock. For the following examples, we use a fictitious stock trading at $50.00 per share. All of the option premiums that are used were calculated using a historical volatility of around .35 (35 percent volatility) on the underlying security with no dividend yield and an interest rate of about 1.45 percent.

MARRIED PUT TECHNIQUE
The Standard Married Put

This technique is the most basic form of the married put trade that was shown in Chapter 1. In a standard married put, you would purchase 100 shares of stock while at the same time purchasing a one month out, out-of-the-money put option.

Standard Married Put from Chapter 1

Buy 100 shares of XYZ at $50.00
Buy to Open 1 contract 1 month out 45 put for $0.50.
(Refer to Figure 1.6 for graphical profit/loss)

The standard married put is essentially a hit or miss trade. The cost of insurance is very small which means the break even is fairly low. The stock needs to gain only $0.50 for the trade to break even. If the stock moves up significantly in the next 30 days, you will realize a profit similar to purchasing shares of stock without the protective put in place. If the stock falls below $45.00, the put can be exercised and the shares of stock will be sold for an 11 percent loss. You could also sell to close the put option or hold the stock and purchase another put option for the next expiration month if you still had a bullish sentiment on the stock. You could also follow those steps if the stock remained between $45.00 and $50.00 at expiration (in Chapter 7 we will go through a thorough discussion of the management techniques for these positions).

Advantages of the Standard Married Put:

- The cost for the protective put is fairly inexpensive.
- The trade is protected for 30 days without sacrificing too much potential profit.

Disadvantages of the Standard Married Put:

- The protection is only for a one month time period.
- If the stock falls in that first month, you will exercise the put and lock in a loss.
- Although you only suffered an 11 percent loss, that is still significant.
- Since the put option is near term, there are not many useful management techniques. The stock can either:
  - Rise in price above the break even for a profit.
  - Remain between $45.00 and $50.00, possibly resulting in a small loss.
  - Drop below $45.00 per share, forcing you to exercise the put for the full loss on the trade.

The standard married put would work best if you were expecting a large increase in the stock price over a short period of time, but also wished to protect against any major declines from an unforeseen market event. The insurance of the purchased put does not take effect until the stock drops below $45.00, but you still have 11 percent at risk. This first married put technique does protect against a major decline in the stock price, but there are better neutral to bullish options strategies you can use to profit on a quick moving stock.

Buying Protective Put Options Further Out in Time

If you were comfortable with this minimal protection but you wanted more time for the stock to go in the desired direction, you could purchase the out-of-the-money put further out in time. When you purchased insurance for your home or entered into an insurance policy for your car, did you shop around first? Of course you did. You wanted to find the best possible coverage for the most discounted price. Once you found the insurance company that suited your needs, you were also able to get a discounted rate if you chose to pay semi-annually or annually rather than month by month. Guess what? The same discounts apply when you are buying put options to protect your shares of stock.

Refer briefly back to Figure 1.4, the option chain for a fictitious stock trading at $50.00 per share. The one month out (30-day), 50 strike call option was trading at $1.55 per contract. The four month out (120-day), 50 strike call option as trading at $3.10 per share. The premium for the further out option is twice the amount of the near term call, but the extra cost is not linear; the further out option is four times further out in time but not four times the cost. If you were trading a strategy where you purchased the one month out option every month for a year, your annualized cost would be $18.60.

$$\$1.55 * 12 \text{ months} = \$18.60$$

You could reduce your annualized cost by purchasing the four month out option. You would only have to pay $3.10 three times over the course of a year for an annualized cost of $9.30.

$3.10 * 3 total purchases every 4 months

Your annualized cost of purchasing the far out option is 50 percent less than if you purchase the one month out option every month.

How far out in time is a long call or long put speculative options investor willing to purchase? You may get a wide range of answers, but you will find that almost all are buying options at least three months, six months, or even twelve months out in time. The further out positions allow more time for the stock to move in the desired direction, but the speculators are not paying three times the near month premium, six times the near month premium, or twelve times the near month premium for the extra time. Yes, the total premium is higher, but the cost per day, or annualized cost, is much lower when an investor purchases options that are further out in time. This fundamental concept of options trading not only applies to speculative long option traders; it also applies to the conservative investor that is using protective strategies.

Another advantage of purchasing options further out in time is rate of time decay. Time decay is the amount of premium that the option will lose over the expiration time period. Options will decay faster as you get closer to expiration. Also, options that are further out in time are not as subjected to daily fluctuations in the stock price compared to nearer term options. Longer-term options typically have a delay, or lag time, when the stock shifts in price during the trading day. If a stock was down a point or two near the close, then opened the next morning a point or two up, you would not see as significant of a change in the price of the far out options as you would be able to notice on the options in the current expiration month. The daily noise of minor price changes in the stock will be filtered out if you are in a longer-term options position, but this can also be a drawback that we will discuss in the next section.

Further Out in Time Standard Married Put

This technique consists of purchasing shares of stock at $50.00 per share and at the same time purchasing the 6-month out, out-of-the-money 45 strike put. This is essentially the same trade as the standard married put trade, but you are purchasing the option further out in time to lower your annualized insurance cost while at the same time giving you more time for the stock to move in your desired direction.

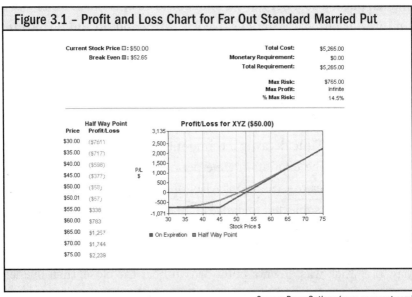

Figure 3.1 – Profit and Loss Chart for Far Out Standard Married Put

Source: PowerOptions (www.poweropt.com)

6-month out Standard Married Put

Buy 100 shares of XYZ at $50.00
Buy to Open 1 contract, 6 month out 45 strike put at $2.65

In the near month, standard married put trade, the 45 strike put would have cost $0.50 per contract. The same strike, 6 month out put costs $2.65. You have gained 6 months of time for the stock to move in your desired direction but you have not paid 6 times the cost of the near month 45 strike put option. Assuming the stock remained at the same price over a 6 month period, you would have paid $3.00 total if you purchased the near month 45 strike put every month for protection. That might seem insignificant since you are only saving $0.35 when you compare it to the cost of the 6 month out put option, but that $0.35 is almost a 12 percent discount.

One of the main problems with this technique is the same one that was shown for the standard married put trade. You have purchased an out-of-the-money put which means the insurance won't 'kick in' until the stock drops below $45.00 per share. If the stock falls below $45.00 at any time between when you entered the trade and 6 months out in time, you could simply exercise the put option. This would give you a loss of 14.5 percent of the capital you used to enter the trade. You are still risking a fairly large percentage of your capital even with the protection in place.

Advantages of Far Out in Time, Standard Married Put:

- You are risking less than 15 percent of your total investment.
- You have six months for the stock to move in the desired direction.
- You have six months to manage the position and cover the cost of the put.

Disadvantages of Far Out in Time, Standard Married Put:

- 15 percent is still a large at risk amount of your capital.
- The insurance is not really a factor unless the stock drops below $45.00.
- If the stock stagnates, you may be 'watching the paint dry' for a few months.

You could also choose to go further than six months out in time. If the stock you were researching has LEAPS options available, you may be able to purchase a put option one year or more out in time. By purchasing an out-of-the-money put option one year out in time, your cost basis and break even would be higher, but you would significantly lower the insurance cost per day.

12 month out OTM Put Option

Buy 100 shares of XYZ at $50.00
Buy to Open 1 contract, 12 month out 45 strike put at $4.30
Total Cost = $54.30 (which is also the break even at expiration)
Maximum Risk = $9.30 per share ($930 for 100 shares)
Percent Maximum Risk = 17.1 percent

We do not need to show a profit and loss chart for this position. Simply picture the previous profit and loss charts with the maximum risk at $930 instead of $765 if the stock was trading below $45.00 at expiration, and a break even at $54.30 for this trade instead of at $52.65. The maximum risk for the out-of-the-money 45 strike protective put is higher for 12 month expiration period, but the daily cost of insurance is lower.

Table 3.1: Cost of Protection per Day Comparison for 45 Strike Put

Expiration Time Period	Ask Price (Time Value)	Cost of Protection per Day
1 month – 30 days	$0.50	$0.017
6 month – 180 days	$2.65	$0.015
1 year – 365 days	$4.30	$0.012

In addition to the overall daily cost of insurance being lower, you would now have twelve months for the stock to move in the desired direction, manage the position to limit any losses if the stock moves down, or sell calls against the stock to generate income and lower the overall cost basis of the married put trade. Also, the far out put options will not have as large of a percentage time decay as the near term option. Despite those advantages, the out-of-the-money, one year out in time married put trade still has the one glaring disadvantage from the standard married put trade using the near month or the six month out in time put: the put insurance does not really start to protect the position until the stock drops below $45.00 per share.

The In-the-Money (ITM) Married Put

In this married put strategy you would purchase 100 shares of stock and at the same time purchase an in-the-money near term put option.

Near Month ITM: (Standard ITM Put Option)

Buy 100 Shares of XYZ at $50.00
Buy to Open 1 contract, 1 month out 55 put for $6.00

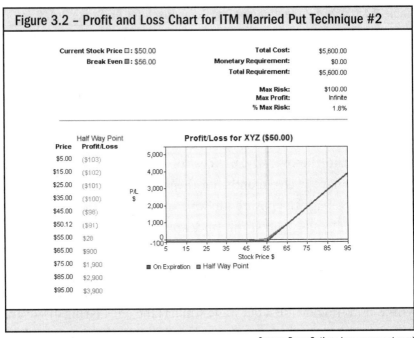

Figure 3.2 – Profit and Loss Chart for ITM Married Put Technique #2

Current Stock Price □: $50.00		Total Cost:	$5,600.00
Break Even ■: $56.00		Monetary Requirement:	$0.00
		Total Requirement:	$5,600.00
		Max Risk:	$100.00
		Max Profit:	Infinite
		% Max Risk:	1.8%

Half Way Point

Price	Profit/Loss
$5.00	($103)
$15.00	($102)
$25.00	($101)
$35.00	($100)
$45.00	($98)
$50.12	($91)
$55.00	$28
$65.00	$900
$75.00	$1,900
$85.00	$2,900
$95.00	$3,900

Profit/Loss for XYZ ($50.00)

■ On Expiration ■ Half Way Point

Source: PowerOptions (www.poweropt.com)

The profit and loss chart is essentially the same, though the break even is much higher. The in-the-money 55 put costs $6.00 per contract, making the overall cost basis $56.00 per share. You would now need the stock to rise above $56.00 (a 12 percent increase in the next 30 days) in order to realize a profit. Your maximum risk on the position is much lower in comparison to the standard married put because the in-the-money put has five points of intrinsic value. You have the right to sell your shares of stock at $55.00 on or before the expiration date. You are only at risk for $1.00 per share on the entire trade, as the total cost basis was $56.00 per share.

But, in order to make a profit or break even, the stock would need to gain 12 percent in just 30 days. Even if the stock moved up to $56.00

per share in 30 days, your put would expire worthless. You h
percent increase on the stock but you did not make a profit on the
trade. You now have to decide if you simply want to sell the shares of
stock at $56.00 or hold on to the stock and purchase another put for
the next expiration month so you still have insurance in place. This
would add to your total cost basis so you will need a further increase
in the stock to make a profit.

Advantages of the ITM Married Put:

- The in-the-money put option will offer a much lower
  maximum risk.

Disadvantages of the ITM Married Put:

- The protection is only for a one month time period.
- If the stock falls in that first month, you can exercise the
  put and lock in a loss.
- The $1.00 per share loss, or 1.8 percent, is small, but it is
  still a loss.
- You need a very large gain in the stock over a very short
  time to make a profit.

Although the in-the-money, near term married put technique has a
limited maximum risk, there is a very small probability that the stock
will have a large enough gain to make a profit. If you were that bullish on the stock and expected a 12 percent increase in a one-month
period, you could make a larger profit by risking less capital trading
long calls or some other leveraged bullish position. Those positions
are not protected, but you would have a better chance of making a
profit in a 30 day period compared to trading a one month out, in-
the-money put. We do not recommend that any investor use this

technique if they are looking for protection while still being in a position to generate income on the stock position because the cost of the insurance is too high.

Recommended Married Put Setup

There are few major points that should stand out from these comparisons:

1. The in-the-money married put had much lower maximum risk than the standard married put.

2. Options that are further out in time have a lower cost of ownership per day.

3. As we said in Chapter 1, the market as a whole will gain roughly 10 percent per year.

With these concepts in mind, we can piece together that an in-the-money, further out in time put would give us a comparatively lower maximum risk with a lower cost per day compared to the near month put positions. This is similar to the protective married put method advocated by Kurt Frankenburg of RadioActive Trading.

6-month out ITM Put Option

Buy 100 Shares of XYZ at $50.00
Buy 1 contract, 6 month out 55 strike put for $7.75

The ITM, near term 55 strike put would have cost you $6.00 per contract. The same strike, 6 month out put option would cost you $7.75. You have gained five months of time for the stock to move in your desired direction but you have not paid five times the cost of the near month 55 strike put option. You only would have paid an extra $1.75 for an additional 150 days of protection.

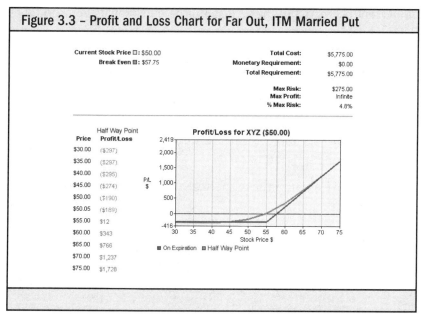

Figure 3.3 – Profit and Loss Chart for Far Out, ITM Married Put

Current Stock Price ☐: $50.00					Total Cost:	$5,775.00
Break Even ■: $57.75					Monetary Requirement:	$0.00
					Total Requirement:	$5,775.00
					Max Risk:	$275.00
					Max Profit:	Infinite
					% Max Risk:	4.8%

Half Way Point

Profit/Loss for XYZ ($50.00)

Price	Profit/Loss
$30.00	($297)
$35.00	($297)
$40.00	($295)
$45.00	($274)
$50.00	($190)
$50.05	($189)
$55.00	$12
$60.00	$343
$65.00	$766
$70.00	$1,237
$75.00	$1,728

■ On Expiration ■ Half Way Point

Source: PowerOptions (www.poweropt.com)

The most you would have at risk in this example is $275.00, or 4.8 percent, over the next 180 days. You have purchased the right to sell your shares of stock at $55.00 at any time between now and the expiration date. Think about that: the stock could have a 20 percent, 25 percent, even a 30 percent drop at any time but you could not lose more than 4.8 percent of the initial investment amount. You have 180 days to manage the position or generate income to help pay for the cost of the insurance and increase the potential return. Another thing to keep in mind is that on average, the expectation is that the market will gain about 10 percent each year. If we are in a married put position that has 6 months to expiration with only a 4.8 percent maximum risk, we might expect to see a 5 percent overall market gain in that 6 month period. Again, the market does not always gain

10 percent per year, but that is just another reason why you should be using these protective strategies in your portfolio.

Advantages of Far Out, ITM Married Put:

- Low risk, great protection over an extended period of time.

- You have six months for the stock to move in the desired direction.

- You have six months to manage the position and cover the cost of the put.

Disadvantages of Far Out, ITM Married Put:

- If the stock stagnates, you may be "watching the paint dry" for a few months.

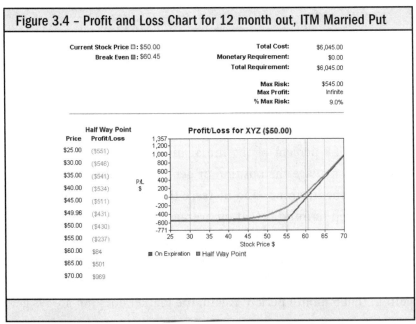

Figure 3.4 – Profit and Loss Chart for 12 month out, ITM Married Put

Source: PowerOptions (www.poweropt.com)

- At face value, you may still need a five or seven percent increase in the stock over the next six months, but proper management techniques can more than cover it.

You could also go further out in time and look to purchase a one year or more in-the-money put. You would have to pay more premium at the time you entered the trade, but the insurance cost per day would be lower and you would now have 12 months to manage or generate income against the position.

12 month out ITM Put Option

Buy 100 Shares of XYZ at $50.00
Buy 1 contract, 12 month out 55 strike put for $10.45

In this example you would have paid $10.45 per contract for the 1 year out, 55 strike put. Your total cost basis would be $60.45 per share, but you can sell to close your stock at $55.00 at any time over the next 12 months. You are only at risk for $5.45 per share, or 9 percent of the initial investment cost for the next 365 days. Just as we saw before, your total cost of protection per day is much lower when you purchase a protective put option further out in time

Table 3.2: Cost of Protection per Day, 55 strike put (including intrinsic value)

Expiration Time Period	Option Ask Price	Total Cost of Protection per Day
1 month – 30 days	$6.00	$0.20
6 month – 180 days	$7.75	$0.04
1 year – 365 days	$10.45	$0.02

With this technique you are able to have the lowest potential risk on your investment, you have lowered the total cost of insurance per day, and you now have an extended time frame to manage the position to increase your potential profits. This is the recommended technique for trading married put positions. You want to look for opportunities where the put option is at least one or more strikes in-the-money, six months to a year out in time with a maximum risk of less than 10 percent. If you look for options that are too deep in-the-money, say greater than 25 percent or more (typically 3 strikes or more depending on the stock price), you may not be in the best position to manage the trade or earn a profit. We will discuss the concerns of going too deep in-the-money in Chapter 4 and Chapter 5.

The At-the-Money Married Put

The next technique we want to analyze is the at-the-money, near month married put position. You may have begun to see the factors that we are using to compare these potential techniques.

1. What is the maximum risk for the position?

2. What is the break even for the position?

3. What is the probability that the stock will reach the break even point?

We wanted to put the at-the-money comparison last in the near month techniques. Many investors may look at the at-the-money put option first thinking, "I paid $50.00 for the stock, why wouldn't I just buy the $50.00 strike put so that I am not risking more than my purchase price?" We're glad that you asked.

In Chapter 1, we outlined the concepts of time value and intrinsic value. Time value was defined as the dollar amount the option buyer is paying for the time until the expiration date and the amount the option seller is collecting for the time to expiration. In the "Putting

Concepts Together" note in that section, it was shown how the at-the-money options have the most time premium for any given expiration month. This means you will pay more per day for the at-the-money put option insurance. We won't show the profit and loss chart for the at-the-money, near month married put trade, but we still need to evaluate the risk and potential.

Near Month ATM: (Standard ATM Put Option)

Buy 100 Shares of XYZ at $50.00
Buy to Open 1 contract, 1 month out 50 put for $2.24
Total Cost = $52.24 (which is also the break even)
Maximum Risk = $2.24
Percent Maximum Risk = 4.3 percent

If the stock gains 4.3 percent in the next 30 days, you will break even on the trade. If it rises more than 4.3 percent, you will make a profit. The percentage time value, the percentage amount that you would pay for the at-the-money put option, is much higher than the previous techniques discussed.

Table 3.3: Percentage Time Value Comparison of Near Month Puts

Put Strike	Put Ask Price	Time Value ($)	% Time Value (of stock price)
45	$0.50	$0.50 (no intrinsic)	1 percent
50	$2.24	$2.24 (no intrinsic)	4.5 percent
55	$6.00	$1.00 (intrinsic = 5)	2 percent

If you purchased the at-the-money protective put option, you would have paid twice as much time premium compared to the in-the-money protective put, and over four times the time premium compared to the out-of-the-money protective put. If the stock stagnated at $50.00 and you decided to keep purchasing at-the-money put options month by month, your annualized cost for the protection would be extremely high. Although it is highly unlikely, let's assume a scenario where this stock remains right at $50.00 over the next year. You decide to keep the stock, but each month you purchase a new put option, as you still want the added protection.

Assuming that volatility remains the same over the course of the year, you would pay $0.50 per month if you were purchasing the out-of-the-money put option every expiration cycle. Your annualized cost of insurance would be $6.00.

$$\$0.50 * 12 \text{ months} = \$6.00$$

By the end of the year your total cost basis on the position would be $56.00. With the stock still trading at $50.00, you would have an unrealized loss of 12 percent.

$$\frac{\$56 \text{ cost basis} - \$50 \text{ price of stock}}{\$50 \text{ price of stock}} = \frac{\$6 \text{ loss}}{\$50 \text{ current price}} = 12\% \text{ loss}$$

If you were following the at-the-money married put position, you would pay roughly $2.24 per month. Your annualized cost of insurance would be $26.88.

$$\$2.24 * 12 = \$26.88$$

Ouch. After 12 months your total cost basis would be $76.88, meaning you would have over a 50 percent loss on the position!

$$\frac{\$76.88 \text{ cost basis} - \$50 \text{ current price}}{\$50 \text{ current price}} = \frac{\$26.88 \text{ loss}}{\$50 \text{ current price}} = 54\% \text{ loss}$$

Let's not even consider the loss you might realize if you purchased the in-the-money put option month by month over the course of the year. We simply wanted to illustrate the potential annualized cost of insurance in the examples that were discussed. You most likely would have gotten out of this position in the first few months if the stock had simply stayed at $50.00 per share. There are other opportunities available where you could earn a profit and you would not tie up your capital in one position for one year if there was no movement in the stock.

COLLAR STRATEGIES

The Standard Collar Spread

Let's not forget the other protective strategy that can be used in an uncertain market. The collar spread strategy has many possible combinations as well because you are combining two options against the same underlying security. In the collar spread strategy, you still have the protection in place from the purchased put, but you are also going to generate income by selling a call against the shares of the underlying stock. The rules and concepts discussed in the married put techniques above also apply to the collar spread strategy. If you choose to purchase near term put options when constructing your collar spread, the annualized cost of insurance will be much higher. Trading near term collar spreads is essentially a hit or miss trade, similar to the standard married put.

Standard Collar Spread

Buy 100 shares of XYZ at $50.00
Sell to Open 1 contract, 1 month out 55 call for $0.60
Buy to Open 1 contract, 1 month out 45 put for $0.50
(Refer to Figure 1.7 for a graphical profit/loss)

We refer to this position as the standard collar spread trade because this is the most common setup you will see in any options investment book or on an educational options website. In this example, you would purchase 100 shares of stock at $50.00, purchase one contract out-of-the-money 45 strike put for $0.50, while at the same time sell one contract out-of-the-money 55 strike call for $0.60. You basically place the standard married put trade, but then sell an out-of-the-money call, which pays for the put option but at the same time caps your potential gains.

When you sell the call option, you are agreeing to sell your shares of stock at the strike price of the call. If the stock gains in value and is trading at $60.00 per share, $65.00 per share, or even $100.00 per share, you will still be obligated to sell your shares of stock at $55.00. If you were assigned at expiration and sold your shares of stock for $55.00, you would still have a 10.2 percent return on the trade. The maximum risk for the standard collar trade is slightly lower than the maximum risk on the standard married put trade.

The $0.60 premium that you collected for selling the call pays for the purchased put option and lowers your cost basis. For this stock, your maximum risk on the standard married put was $5.50 per share (10.9 percent) and the maximum risk on the standard collar spread is $4.90 per share (9.8 percent).

In the standard collar spread, you still only have 30 days for the stock to move up above $55.00 per share so you can realize the maximum return. The return on this trade is not unlimited, as it was with the standard married put position. A 10.2 percent return over a 30 day period is very respectable, but you will only realize that return if the stock is trading above $55.00 (a 10 percent increase) in the next 30 days. Because both options have a near term expiration date, there are not a lot of profitable or reliable management techniques that can be applied short of rolling both options out to the next expiration month.

Advantages of Standard Collar Spread:

- The premium received from selling the call option pays for the cost of the put.
- The trade is decently protected for the next 30 days.
- If the stock stays between the strike prices and both options expire, you still collected a slight net credit ($0.10 in this example) to cover commission costs.

Disadvantages of Standard Collar Spread:

- The protection is only for a one month time period.
- If the stock falls in that first month, you will exercise the put and lock in a loss.
- Although you only suffered a 9.8 percent loss, it is still a loss.
- At expiration you will either:
    - Hopefully get assigned and realize the 10.2 percent return.
    - Have both options expire and have to enter a collar for the next month.
    - Exercise the put option for the maximum loss if the stock is below $45.00 at expiration.

Just like the standard married put position, this collar spread technique works best if you are expecting a large gain in the stock price over a short period of time, but you still wish to have some protection in place in case of a major unforeseen market event. However, this technique is still a hit or miss 30 day protective strategy.

You may be wondering how the profit/loss would look if you sold the at-the-money 50 strike call while purchasing the 45 strike put. Well, let's take a look at the mathematical risk and returns of that potential combination:

Standard Collar Spread: Call At-the-Money

Buy stock XYZ at $50.00
Sell to Open 1 contract, 1 month out 50 call at $2.15
Buy to Open 1 contract, 1 month out 45 put at $0.50
Total Cost = $48.35 (which is also the break even at expiration)
Maximum Risk = $3.35 per share ($335 for 100 shares)
Percent Maximum Risk = 6.9 percent
Maximum Profit = $1.65 ($165 for 100 shares)
Percent Maximum Profit = 3.4 percent

Selling the at-the-money call option has lowered the maximum return and only slightly lowered the percent maximum risk. Even though you would have collected a higher premium for selling the at-the-money option, you would not take advantage of the additional appreciation, as you are obligated to sell the shares of stock at $50.00 per share. You would have a higher probability of getting assigned and earning the 3.4 percent return, and because the at-the-money call option has the largest time premium of the potential calls to sell in the near month, your maximum risk would be lowered as well. This would be a good strategy to use if you expected the stock to stay at the same price or move up slightly over the next 30 days, but you still wished to purchase the protective put to avoid any large declines. However, since both options have only 30 days to expiration, you still do not have many viable management techniques if the stock remains between the strike price of the call option and the put option at expiration or if the stock falls below the put strike price.

As it was with the married put strategy, you can create a collar spread with the put option further out in time to minimize the cost of daily insurance.

The Standard Collar Put Further Out in Time

Let us pause for a moment and take a deep breath. This is a lot of information to absorb in one chapter, but the information is necessary so you can see the potential risk and rewards of each combination. Before we jump back in to the next strategy, let us review again some of the basic concepts that we have seen from the previous examples.

1. Buying in-the-money protective put options offer a much lower maximum risk than the out-of-the-money protective put options.

2. Options that are further out in time have a lower cost per day.

3. Options that are sold in the near term will have a higher premium collected per day.

4. As we said in Chapter 1, the market as a whole will gain roughly 10 percent per year.

Applying these concepts to the aspects of the collar spread strategy give us a guideline for the best potential call and put combinations to use. We would want to purchase a put further out in time to lower the per day cost of the insurance while at the same time sell the near term call option to generate the highest annualized income.

Standard Collar Strikes with Put Option 6 Months Out in Time

Buy 100 shares of XYZ at $50.00
Sell to Open 1 contract, 1 month out 55 strike call at $0.60
Buy to Open 1 contract, 6 months out 45 strike put at $2.40

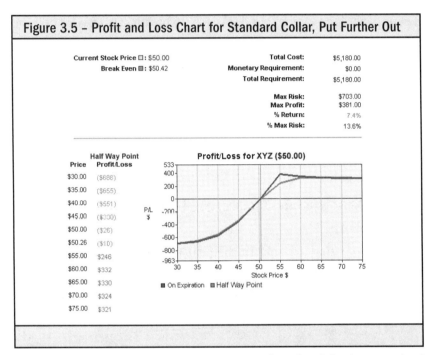

Figure 3.5 – Profit and Loss Chart for Standard Collar, Put Further Out

Current Stock Price □: $50.00		
Break Even ▣: $50.42		

Total Cost:	$5,180.00
Monetary Requirement:	$0.00
Total Requirement:	$5,180.00
Max Risk:	$703.00
Max Profit:	$381.00
% Return:	7.4%
% Max Risk:	13.6%

Half Way Point

Price	Profit/Loss
$30.00	($688)
$35.00	($655)
$40.00	($551)
$45.00	($330)
$50.00	($26)
$50.26	($10)
$55.00	$246
$60.00	$332
$65.00	$330
$70.00	$324
$75.00	$321

Profit/Loss for XYZ ($50.00)

■ On Expiration   ▣ Half Way Point

Source: PowerOptions (www.poweropt.com)

At first glance, this strategy appears to offer no benefit over the standard collar trade. You had to pay more for the far out protective put and you still collected the same premium for selling the near term call option. If the stock moves above $55.00 at the near term expiration, you will be assigned for a return of 6.2 percent. But you will still own the 45 strike put, which is now further out-of-the-money but still has 5 months of time value remaining. You could now sell to close the put option and earn slightly more, or you may decide to repurchase the stock and sell the next month out 60 strike call. Again, the management techniques for the recommended married put and collar spread trades will be discussed in Chapter 7.

If you are not assigned at the near term expiration, you still have the protective put in place and you can now sell another call against the stock. This will allow you to effectively lower your cost basis while still being in a position to generate income if the stock moves up in price. Remember, if you purchased the one month out, 45 strike protective put month by month, your insurance cost per day would be much higher. Purchasing the put further out in time also allows much more flexibility in managing the position over time.

Advantages of Standard Collar with put further out in time:

- The premium received from selling the call option lowers the cost of the put.

- You are maximizing the annual premium received by selling near term, while at the same time lowering the annual cost of protection.

- The trade is decently protected for the next 30 days.

- You can still earn a good return if you are assigned at the near term expiration.

- If the stock stagnates, the call will expire worthless but you still hold the protective put. You can sell a new call for the next expiration and further lower your cost basis.

Disadvantages of Standard Collar with put further out in time:

- The protection does not start to kick in until the stock drops below $45.00.

- The premium received from selling the call does not cover the cost of the put.

- In some situations you may be assigned in the first month for a loss, depending on the cost of the put and the profit earned when you are assigned.

- If the stock stagnates, you may need to hold the stock and the purchased put for several months before a profit can be realized.

Just as with the far out married put comparison, we can also take a look at purchasing the one year out, out-of-the-money 45 strike put while at the same time selling the out-of-the-money near term call option.

Standard Collar Strikes with Put Option 12 Months Out in Time

Buy 100 shares of XYZ at $50.00
Sell to Open 1 contract, 1 month out 55 strike call at $0.60
Buy to Open 1 contract, 12 months out 45 strike put at $4.30
Total Cost = $53.70 per share
Maximum Risk = $3.70 per share ($370 for 100 shares)
Percent Maximum Risk = 6.9 percent
Maximum Profit (near term expiration) = $1.30 ($130 for 100 shares)
Percent Maximum Profit (near term expiration) = 2.4 percent

This return may seem very small, but you have purchased a put option 12 months out in time. If you were assigned at the near term expiration you would still have 11 months of time value remaining on your put option. You could sell to close the put to earn more income or you could repurchase shares of stock, as the protective put is already in place. You have 12 months to manage the position and earn a much higher profit if the stock continues to rise or even if the stock falls in price.

As you learned with the married put techniques, you can lower the maximum risk even more by purchasing an in-the-money put option while at the same time lowering your insurance cost per day by going further out in time.

Debit Collar Spread

How were you able to decrease the maximum risk in the married put techniques? You purchased an in-the-money put for a higher premium, but because of the intrinsic value of the put option, your maximum risk was much lower. The break even price was much higher, meaning you had a lower probability of earning a profit, but you were risking less on the trade. The same scenario can be seen in the debit collar spread.

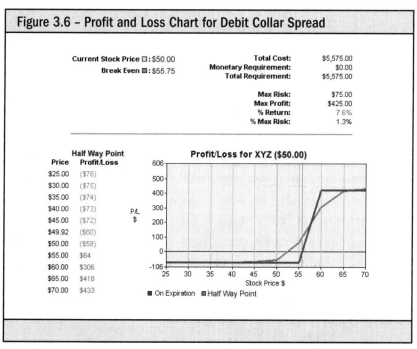

Figure 3.6 – Profit and Loss Chart for Debit Collar Spread

Source: PowerOptions (www.poweropt.com)

Debit Collar Spread

Buy 100 shares of XYZ at $50.00
Sell to Open 1 contract, 1 month out 60 call for $0.25
Buy to Open 1 contract, 1 month out 55 put for $6.00

You have purchased the in-the-money, near term 55 strike put for $6.00 and sold a deep out-of-the-money 60 strike call for $0.25. You would pay a debit of $5.75 because the put option has a much higher price than the premium you received for selling the call. The overall cost basis is $55.75 per share but you have the right to exercise the put and sell your shares of stock for $55.00 any time between now and the expiration date. This makes the maximum risk only $0.75 per share, or 1.3 percent of the total investment amount.

If you are assigned at the call strike price, you can still make a profit of $4.25 per share, or 7.6 percent over a 30 day time period. In order for you to be assigned, the stock would have to be trading above $60.00 per share. You would need a 20 percent increase in the stock price over a 30 day period to realize the 7.6 percent return. This type of collar spread, commonly referred to as a debit collar, does offer a low maximum risk, but there is such a low probability of getting assigned and earning the maximum return that it is not a technique that we recommend. If you expected that large of a gain in the stock over a 30 day period, you could make a larger profit by risking less capital trading long calls or some other leveraged bullish position. Those positions are not protected, but you would have a better chance of making a profit in a 30 day period compared to this collar spread example.

Advantages of the Debit Collar Spread:

- Because you purchased an in-the-money put, the maximum risk is very low.

- You can still earn a 7 percent return in 30 days.

Disadvantages of the Debit Collar Spread:

- The premium from selling the call only covers 4 percent of the put cost.

- Potential profits are capped by the obligation of the sold call.

- You need the stock to move up significantly in only 30 days to break even.

- Since both options expire in 30 days, there are not many management techniques that can be applied, short of rolling both options out and increasing your annualized cost basis.

Remember, these techniques are based on the theoretical premiums of our theoretical stock. Not every collar spread as outlined in one of the debit collar spreads would offer a 7.6 percent return with only a 1.3 percent maximum risk, but the comparison would be similar. You would expect to have a fairly low risk with a relatively high return if assigned due to the appreciation to the higher call strike price, but you would have a very low probability of the stock reaching that price and earning that return.

Without going into too much detail, let's take a quick look at another potential debit dollar spread.

Debit Collar: Buy Put ATM, Sell Call 1 strike OTM

Buy 100 shares of XYZ at $50.00
Sell to Open 1 contract, 1 month out 55 call for $0.60
Buy to Open 1 contract, 1 month out 50 put for $2.24
Total Cost = $51.64 (which is also the break even at expiration)
Maximum Risk = $1.64 per share ($164 for 100 shares)
Percent Maximum Risk = 3.2 percent
Maximum Profit = $3.36 ($336 for 100 shares)
Percent Maximum Profit = 6.5 percent

In this debit collar you have purchased the protective put at-the-money while selling the one strike out-of-the-money call option. The total debit from the options transactions would be $1.64.

$2.24 put ask price - $0.60 call bid price = $1.64 total debit

You would have a limited maximum risk of 3.2 percent with a potential return of about 6.5 percent. Your total at–risk value is slightly higher compared to the first debit collar example and your maximum return has been slightly lowered. The main difference is that in this debit collar spread you have a better chance of getting assigned and earning the 6.5 percent return, as you would only need the stock to rise above $55.00 per share, compared to $60.00 per share in the first example. This strategy can work if you expect the stock to gain 10 percent or more in value in the first 30 days, but you wish to closely protect the initial capital that you used to enter the trade.

Recommended Collar Trade

A debit collar with the put option far out in time will drastically lower your overall risk on the trade while at the same time generate some income to help pay for the cost of the put option. This is the technique the co-authors feel would give you the best protection over time and more choices to manage the position.

Buy ITM Put Option 6 Months Out, Sell Deep OTM Call Near Term

Buy 100 shares of XYZ at $50.00
Sell to Open 1 contract, 1 month out 60 strike call at $0.25
Buy to Open 1 contract, 6 months out 55 strike put at $7.75

In this trade, you have lowered your maximum risk to $2.50, or 4.3 percent of your initial investment amount. You can only lose 4.3 percent at any time between now and 180 days out in time. If the

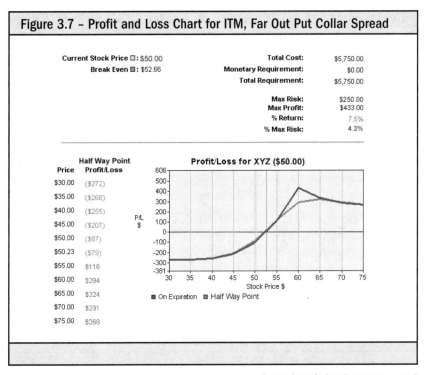

Figure 3.7 – Profit and Loss Chart for ITM, Far Out Put Collar Spread

Current Stock Price □: $50.00

Break Even ■: $52.66

Total Cost:	$5,750.00
Monetary Requirement:	$0.00
Total Requirement:	$5,750.00
Max Risk:	$250.00
Max Profit:	$433.00
% Return:	7.5%
% Max Risk:	4.3%

	Half Way Point
Price	Profit/Loss
$30.00	($272)
$35.00	($268)
$40.00	($255)
$45.00	($207)
$50.00	($87)
$50.23	($79)
$55.00	$116
$60.00	$294
$65.00	$324
$70.00	$291
$75.00	$268

Profit/Loss for XYZ ($50.00)

■ On Expiration ■ Half Way Point

Source: PowerOptions (www.poweropt.com)

stock rises above $60.00 in the next 30 days, you will be assigned for a return of 4.3 percent. However, your put option will still have six months of time value remaining. If you were assigned at near term expiration and had to sell your shares of stock at $60.00, you could still sell to close your put option and increase your return. The calculated maximum profit if assigned, including the remaining time value of the put option, is 7.5 percent. You could also decide to reinvest in the stock since your protective put is already in place.

As discussed in the near month debit collar, you have a very low probability of the stock gaining 20 percent in the first 30 days and getting assigned in the first month. The goal of the protective strategies is maximizing the protection. This collar spread technique offers the lowest potential risk while giving you time to manage the position and earn a respectable return even if the stock remains at $50.00 or drops over the next six months.

Trading Tip – Strategy Comparison

If you are an advanced options investor, you may have noticed that the risk-reward chart for the long term collars, Figure 3.5 and Figure 3.7, are very similar to a Diagonal Calendar Call Spread. The difference between the strategies is that the put option in the collar spreads increases in value as the stock falls, limiting the loss on the position. The long call in a diagonal calendar call spread decreases in value as the stock falls. Although the diagonal calendar call spread is leveraged, you can still lose 30 percent, 40 percent or more of your investment value if the stock has a small decline.

Advantages of Long Term Debit Collar Spread:

- The premium from selling the call option slightly lowers the cost of the put.

- You are maximizing the annual premium received by selling near term, while at the same time lowering the annual cost of protection.

- You have a very limited maximum risk.

- Though unlikely, you can still realize a good return if assigned in the first month.

- You have an extended period of time to manage the position with very low risk.

Disadvantages of Long Term Debit Collar Spread:

- You need a significant increase to realize the initial maximum return.

- The premium from the OTM call may just pay for the commission cost, depending on the number of shares/contracts you trade.

- In some situations, you may be assigned in the first month for a loss, depending on the cost of the put and the profit earned when you are assigned.

- If the stock stagnates, you may need to hold the stock and the purchased put for several months before a profit can be realized.

As we have done before, let's compare this technique using the 12 month put as well.

Buy ITM Put Option 12 Months Out, Sell Deep OTM Call Near Term

Buy 100 shares of XYZ at $50.00
Sell to Open 1 contract, 1 month out 60 strike call at $0.25
Buy to Open 1 contract, 12 months out 55 strike put at $10.45
Total Cost = $60.25 per share
Maximum Risk = $5.25 per share ($525 for 100 shares)
Percent Maximum Risk = 8.7 percent
Maximum Profit (near term expiration) = -$0.25 (loss of $25 for 100 shares)
Percent Maximum Profit (near term expiration) = -0.4 percent

In this combination the static return, if assigned, is negative since the cost basis is greater than the strike price of the sold call. The maximum risk is slightly more than double the previous example. However, in this example you have 12 months to manage the position and realize a profit. If the stock was trading above $60.00 at the near term expiration, you could simply buy to close the short call and cancel the obligation of assignment, then sell to open a new call for the next expiration month. You could also allow the stock to be assigned for the slight loss and then sell to close the put option, as you still have 11 months of time value remaining on the option.

Trading Tip – Other Combinations

You may be wondering why we did not show a collar combination where both options were below the stock price (put OTM, call ITM) or longer term collars using an ITM, far out put for protection but an ATM, near term call for premium. When trading a collar spread it is not recommended to have the sold call strike price below the put strike that you purchased for protection. You can use the tools on PowerOptions to find these spreads and compare the risk-reward against the combinations we have shown in this chapter.

REVIEW

We selected these combinations to give you the basics of the various trades you can create using the married put or the collar spread strategy. Each stock will have a different risk-reward profile depending on the stock and the prices of the put option or the call option. When entering either a married put trade or a collar spread trade you need to compare the maximum risk, the potential return and the likelihood that you will earn that return in the next 30, 60, or 180 days out in time. You want to make sure that you are lowering the maximum risk as much as possible while still keeping in mind the potential of earning a profit on the trade. In some situations, it might be better to sacrifice a near term return to have a much lower maximum risk, while at other times you may wish to sacrifice the lower maximum risk to speculate on a higher near term return. The combination that you select depends on your risk-reward threshold and your expected price movement of the underlying stock.

For the next few chapters we will only focus on the married put and collar spread strategies that are the best suited for the conservative investor focused on limiting the maximum risk. In the next chapter we will review the stock selection criteria that you can use to help identify neutral to bullish stocks.

Chapter 4

SELECTING THE RIGHT STOCKS

The protective strategies discussed in this text are neutral to bullish strategies. The married put strategy is a bullish strategy, as you need the stock to move up in price in order to make a profit. If the stock stagnates, the position will not yield a profit. If you are trading the near term married puts outlined in the previous chapter, you are essentially in a hit or miss position. Using longer term put options will give you more flexibility over time to manage the position. You may have been wrong in the short term, but you should expect to be right in the longer term. The collar spread strategy is a neutral to bullish position because you will be able to generate income and lower the cost basis even if the stock remains at the same price. The maximum profit, however, for any collar spread combination is only achieved if the stock moves up in price. Therefore, it is essential to focus your attention on stocks that have bullish criteria. Even though you may have researched the stock thoroughly and selected a position that you feel will go up in price, there will be times when you are wrong for any number of reasons. You have probably experienced this before, which is why you are considering trading these protective strategies. Since purchasing longer term, in-the-money put options are more protective, you should only look for stocks that you would not mind owning for an extended period of time. If your expectations of the company change during the expiration period and you are no longer bullish on the stock, there are management techniques you can use to limit your loss and further hedge the position. However, at any time you should not be afraid to simply liquidate the entire position if you do not feel the stock will ever recover.

WHAT CRITERIA IDENTIFY A BULLISH STOCK?

There are many criteria used to determine what stocks will go up in price. Most stock analysts use both fundamental and technical criteria in their evaluations. By fundamental, we mean how a company is performing judging from financial measurements like earnings, cash flow, and sales. Technical analysis primarily deals with the chart pattern of the underlying stock. As an example, one might determine if the stock is in an uptrend or at a resistance point, or perhaps hitting new highs. There are some analysts who believe that the fundamentals are already built into the price of the stock and concentrate exclusively on the chart pattern of the stock. While many fundamentalists consider the use of charts paramount to use of voodoo, in reality, both techniques should be used because so many people in each camp follow them. Each makes a contribution to our understanding of what a good company is to maximize the potential gains of the protective strategies.

WHAT DO THE CHARTS TELL US?

Technically, we are looking for a stock that has a rising chart pattern. To discern this trend we generally use a chart program to plot the stock prices over some period of time. Since we are focusing on the protective strategy where the purchased put is six months to a year or more out in time, you might want to focus on a one year chart pattern. This will allow you to see the recent trends of the potential stock as well as see any seasonal weakness or "trouble spots" that the company may have experienced. The charts below show a stock in an uptrend and the contrasting downtrend. Just by looking at the chart you can get a good feel about the trend in stock price with time. These charts show a one year period of time.

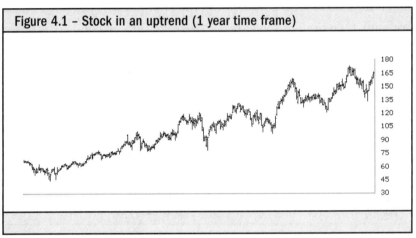

Figure 4.1 – Stock in an uptrend (1 year time frame)

Source: PowerOptions (www.poweropt.com)

This stock shows a continued upward trend over the course of the last year, though there were some spots where the stock had a decline over a short period of time. In the past month, the stock has come out of one such decline, but has started to go back up in price. These declines can actually work to your advantage for two reasons.

1. If you are looking to enter into a married put or collar spread trade, you can buy the stock for a slightly cheaper price during

one of these declines (unfortunately, at that time the put option will be more expensive because the put will increase in value as the stock falls).

2. If you are already in the married put or collar spread trade, the drawdown will give you an opportunity to maneuver your put option or adjust the position to lower your cost basis or to generate income.

In theory, you could maximize your overall cost basis by legging into one of the protective strategies by purchasing the stock after it has fallen in price and then purchasing the put option as the stock moves back up. One of the problems with legging into positions is that you may never see the stock move back up in price. This will leave you holding onto shares of a declining stock without the protection in place. The chart pattern in Figure 4.1 is what you want to look for when entering a married put or a collar spread trade.

Figure 4.2 is the type of pattern that you want to avoid when looking to enter a married put or a collar spread trade. Over the last year the

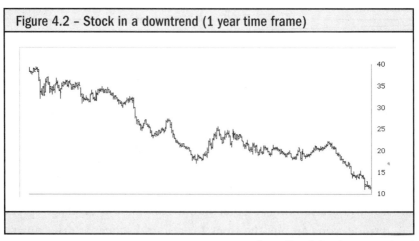

Figure 4.2 - Stock in a downtrend (1 year time frame)

Source: PowerOptions (www.poweropt.com)

stock has dropped from a high of almost $40.00 per share and is currently trading just above $11.50. That's a 71 percent decrease over 12 months! In the last few months this stock has shown a drastic downturn, dropping from a price of about $22.00 to just over $11.00 per share. If you had traded a long-term married put or collar spread on this stock one year ago, you would have greatly reduced your losses. If you were looking to open a protective position today, this would not be the type of stock you would want to trade. You want to look for bullish or neutral stocks that you would not mind holding in your account.

WHAT ARE SOME OF THE WAYS TO IDENTIFY UPTRENDING STOCKS?

The stock in Figure 4.1 is clearly in an uptrend for the last year. One of the ways that an investor can identify these types of stocks is to use the simple moving average (SMA). One of the commonly used filters is to look for stocks that are currently trading above their 50 day moving average.

Figure 4.3 - Stock in an uptrend with SMA 50

Source: PowerOptions (www.poweropt.com)

Figure 4.3 shows the same stock from Figure 4.1 with the SMA 50 line shown as well. The stock is clearly trading above the 50 day moving average, but it is also important to note the periods of time when the stock fell below the SMA 50. Each time the stock approached the SMA 50 or violated the 50 day moving average, the stock rebounded and moved back up in price. You can also use this pattern to determine support levels when entering into a trade.

FUNDAMENTALS TO EXAMINE

Good management is often cited as a prerequisite for a good company, but how do you identify good management? If a manager has a long track record and many years of experience in the company, we can see how the company has performed and attribute the amount of success or failure to that manager. However, managers change frequently and move from company to company, making it more difficult to tell how they will do in the company you are researching. Institutional investors, like the manager of a mutual fund, will often visit a firm they expect to invest in to assess the company. But one must realize that the company will be putting its best foot forward and telling the mutual fund manager what they want to hear. The only real way to know the quality of management is in the results that they have achieved.

Most important in evaluating a company's performance is their sales growth. Everything comes from sales growth. Even if the company is not yet profitable, with strong sales growth, expenses can be cut, operating efficiencies can be improved, and direct costs can be reduced. But without good sales growth a company is always on the defensive. Their cost of goods and expenses will be under constant pressure and growing earnings will be very hard to achieve. Even if expenses can be reduced, there is always a limit to decreasing expenses to improve earnings if the sales are not there also. Therefore, look to top line sales growth of at least 15 to 20 percent.

Companies are generally valued by their ability to generate earnings. The sales growth should improve earnings at an increasing rate. As sales grow, the earnings increases should be easier and easier to achieve. One of the measures investors look at is a stock's price to earnings ratio. Therefore, as the earnings increase, we would expect the price to move up also. In fact, if the earnings growth is rapid enough, the price to earnings ratio may increase because the company will be perceived as outperforming. This can often increase the price of the stock very rapidly, as it will be driven not only by the earnings growth but also by the price to earnings ratio. Look for a string of increased earnings over the last few years and most importantly, increases over the last few quarters. Earnings should increase at least as fast as sales or faster. In general, if you want to earn 20 percent per year from your investments, then the earnings of your holdings must grow at that rate or greater to succeed over the long run. It is just unreasonable to expect your stock to go up if it is not supported by strong earnings growth.

William O'Neil of *Investors Business Daily* likes companies that have something new in their outlook. Consider favorably a company with a new product, new management, or a new high in the price of the stock, something that will bring positive attention to the stock and help drive its price per share higher. This added attention could cause brokers to increase their recommendations on the stock and encourage institutions like mutual funds to increase their purchase of the stock. Both of these effects will help move the stock up in price. Institutions are a major source of volume in today's market. Increases in volume are indicative of institutional activity. This high volume activity with increasing prices will attract more institutions and often start a buying frenzy. Again, you are looking for events that will help move the price of the stock in a positive direction.

It is also good to invest in stocks that are favored by the institutions. Certain groups or sectors are favored at different times in the market cycle, while others may fall out of favor. While oil prices are going up, oil, gas, and drilling companies will be very hot, but airlines and trucking may not be so popular because their costs are going up with the price of fuel. It is easier for your stock to go up if it is in a popular industry. But even more important than the group the stock is in is the overall market environment. Generally, three quarters of any upward movement in stock price comes from the overall market. Everything tends to move together. It is much more difficult for your stock to go up when the overall market is declining. Therefore, try to do your stock buying when the market is strong and trending upward. Use a general index like the S&P 500 as a broad gauge on the health of the market. As an example, if the S&P 500 is above its 50 day moving average, the market is probably in an uptrend and your stock of interest will be in an uptrend. The trend is your friend, so keep it positive.

WHAT HAVE WE ACHIEVED?

Can we now guarantee that our stock selected by using these steps will not go down? Absolutely not! No matter how careful we are, there will be some cases where the stock falls. That is the advantage of using the protective strategies over leveraged or speculative options investment strategies. By entering the married put position you can limit your maximum risk to only seven percent or less of your invested capital. If the stock drops, you still have the protection in place and you can use various management techniques to put yourself in a more protected position.

We owned shares in a healthcare stock that was a leader in the industry, it had a great earnings record, and the stock price had been moving up to the right for many months. How could you go wrong? Well, it went wrong. Over the next month, this stock declined by more than 10 percent because the company was in the process of being audited by the SEC for backdating insider company stock option awards. Now, an event like this had nothing to do with the company's financials or earnings. It had nothing to do with the company's competitive position in the industry or with future industry prospects. But the stock went down on the potential threat of an audit. Even with the protection in place, we actually looked at the decline in stock price as an opportunity to buy. We will discuss the management techniques when a stock declines in later chapters, but we wanted to emphasize that things do not always go as planned. Although in this case, the stock eventually returned to its previous price and we were very well rewarded for taking advantage of this short-term dislocation in the market.

A BETTER APPROACH

It could take many hours in the library, visits to companies, or work on the internet to find some good prospects. But we do not all have the time and energy necessary to do the research. Just how practical is it to investigate all of these criteria to find a good stock? There were over 3,300 optionable stocks, ETFs and indexes at the time this text was written. The process of doing the necessary research to seek out the best companies can be accomplished in another way. Consider using an online interactive screening tool to search for your investment opportunities. One such tool is the SmartSearchXL tool provided at www.poweropt.com.

The SmartSearchXL Tool

This tool will allow a user to search the entire universe of optionable stocks and all of their 300,000 options to find the ones that meet a certain criteria. The search criteria can be earnings growth, market capitalization, Z score, broker recommendations, if the stock is in an uptrend and a variety of other parameters. Therefore, fundamen-

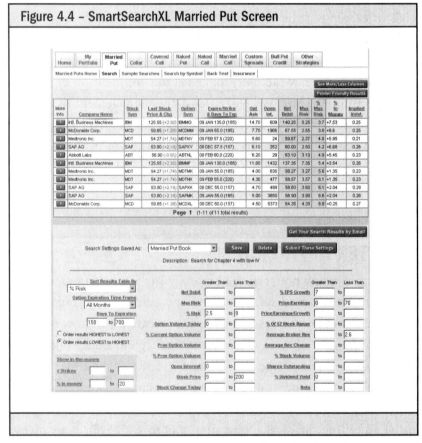

Figure 4.4 – SmartSearchXL Married Put Screen

Source: PowerOptions (www.poweropt.com)

tal financial parameters, technical chart information, and industry group or market trends can be all monitored and searched simultaneously. Hours of research in the library can be reduced to several clicks and a few minutes with a powerful tool like this. Someone not on Wall Street can now reduce what was once a full time job to a part time activity.

Figure 4.4 shows the married put results for different positions.

Basic Option Criteria:

- Between 150 days (5 months) and 700 days (about two years) out in time.

- Less than 20 percent in the money. If the put is too deep in-the-money, you will not be able to manage the position effectively. It is unlikely that the stock will gain close to 20 percent in the next few months or even in the next year.

- Limited between a 2.5 and 9 percent maximum risk. The goal of the protective strategies is to limit the maximum risk. Some of the positions with a very low maximum risk may be too deep in the money to manage correctly.

- Option volume greater than 0. This will allow us to see only those options that have at least 1 contract bought or sold today. In most options strategies you might want to look for a much higher daily option volume when you are entering the trade. However, the far out options do not have a lot of activity, as most of the option activity is on the near term expiration months.

- Open interest greater than 0. This is another measure of liquidity in the market. A general rule is to have the open interest at least 5 times the number of contracts you want to trade. Again, you have to consider that the far out options do not have a lot of activity and we do not want to filter out too many positions if the risk-reward criteria are met.

Stock Criteria:

- Earnings growth greater than 7 percent. Remember, we wanted to be sure the company was growing its earnings at about the rate of return we were seeking.

- Price/earnings ratio between 0 and 70. This ratio reflects the current price of the stock divided by the earnings. In addition to screening for strong earnings growth, you also do not want the stock price to be inordinately high compared to the earnings.

- Broker recommendation less than 2.6 (1 is best). This setting is looking for brokers to look at this stock in a generally favorable light. The lower the number, the better the rating. This parameter is not shown in the results above to keep the output simple.

- Dividend yield (percent) greater than 0. This allows you only to see stocks that pay a dividend. Many consider stocks that pay a dividend to be strong growth companies. In either of the protective strategies, you have to purchase shares of stock, which means you will receive the dividend if the company pays a dividend. The extra income may seem slight depending on the company, but a little extra money never hurts.

- Market capitalization greater than one billion. Many investors prefer to trade only on mid or large cap stocks. This setting means the system will only find the large cap stocks that match the rest of the criteria. Large cap stocks have a tendency to hold their value even in market downturns, though you should not assume that large cap stocks always increase in value.

- Average stock volume greater than 300,000 shares per day. This allows you to filter for the liquidity of the stock. Only those stocks that trade at least 300,000 shares per day on average (over the last 30 days) will appear in the results. Stocks with a low average volume may have a tendency to stagnate or slip in price over time. If there were no interest in the stock, why would you expect the shares to increase in value?

- Stocks greater than their 50 day moving average (box not shown). This allows you to find only those stocks that are in an uptrend as discussed earlier. Using this filter will help you save research time. You still want to check the chart of the stocks that appear in the results, but you have already filtered out those stocks that are in a downtrend compared to their 50 day moving average.

- Stock prices between $9 and $200. This filter is a personal preference and depends on the amount of available capital in your account. You still need to purchase shares of stock in order to enter one of the protective strategies. If you are only allocating $10,000 to enter new positions, you might want to lower the upper stock price limit.

There were eleven positions that met these requirements on five different stocks. This search took just a few seconds to scan for stock prices, fundamentals, technical trends, and option risk all at the same time. In addition to the filters that were outlined, you could also use the SmartSearchXL tool to filter stocks by: RSI, Bollinger Bands, Beta, Stock Volatility, 52 Week Range, Stock Change Today (by monetary value or percentage), Price/Earnings Ratio, Shares Outstanding and several other fundamental and technical criteria.

You can also screen specifically against a given sector or industry or remove (filter out) a specific sector or industry. If you have a specific list of stocks that you follow, you can also create your own personal stock list and look for protective positions against only those companies. The results in the example search were filtered by the lowest maximum risk to the highest. You can select to order the results by any of the criteria that are available for the given strategy. You can also customize the view of the results table so you are only seeing the data that applies to the criteria you might use to analyze a position.

Once you have run your search, should you automatically place the trade that appears at the top of the results? Of course not, you want to further research the underlying stock to make sure that you are comfortable with the trading history and that there are no outstanding events that may be a problem in the future. The first column on the results table to the left of each trade is labeled "More Info." The More Info key will give you access to additional information about each of the stock selections presented in the results table. The More Info key is basically a one-stop shop for everything you would need to know about a company.

Figure 4.5 – The More Information Menu

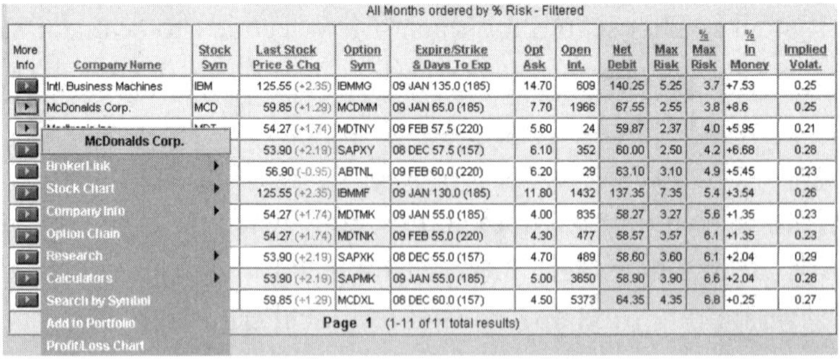

All Months ordered by % Risk - Filtered

More Info	Company Name	Stock Sym	Last Stock Price & Chg	Option Sym	Expire/Strike & Days To Exp	Opt Ask	Open Int.	Net Debit	Max Risk	% Max Risk	% In Money	Implied Volat.
▶	Intl. Business Machines	IBM	125.55 (+2.35)	IBMMO	09 JAN 135.0 (185)	14.70	609	140.25	5.25	3.7	+7.53	0.25
▶	McDonalds Corp.	MCD	59.85 (+1.29)	MCDMM	09 JAN 65.0 (185)	7.70	1966	67.55	2.55	3.8	+8.6	0.25
▶	Medtronic Inc.	MDT	54.27 (+1.74)	MDTNY	09 FEB 57.5 (220)	5.60	24	59.87	2.37	4.0	+5.95	0.21
▶	McDonalds Corp.			SAPXY	08 DEC 57.5 (157)	6.10	352	60.00	2.50	4.2	+6.68	0.28
▶	BrokerLink			ABTNL	09 FEB 60.0 (220)	6.20	29	63.10	3.10	4.9	+5.45	0.23
▶	Stock Chart			IBMMF	09 JAN 130.0 (185)	11.80	1432	137.35	7.35	5.4	+3.54	0.26
▶	Company Info			MDTMK	09 JAN 55.0 (185)	4.00	835	58.27	3.27	5.8	+1.35	0.23
▶	Option Chain			MDTNK	09 FEB 55.0 (220)	4.30	477	58.57	3.57	6.1	+1.35	0.23
▶	Research			SAPXK	08 DEC 55.0 (157)	4.70	489	58.60	3.60	6.1	+2.04	0.29
▶	Calculators			SAPMK	09 JAN 55.0 (185)	5.00	3650	58.90	3.90	6.6	+2.04	0.28
▶	Search by Symbol			MCDXL	08 DEC 60.0 (157)	4.50	5373	64.35	4.35	6.8	+0.25	0.27
	Add to Portfolio		Page 1 (1-11 of 11 total results)									
	Profit/Loss Chart											

Source: PowerOptions (www.poweropt.com)

In Figure 4.5, for McDonald's Corp., clicking on the More Info button produces a list other information specifically about this company.

- **Broker Link**—provides access to the order page of a broker, if you want to place that trade. We will discuss this feature in more detail later in the book.

- **Stock Chart**—displays a customizable chart similar to the ones shown above.

- **Company Info**—provides information on company specific news, earnings and events like splits or dividends, and a company profile, which highlights the company's business with financials.

- **Option Chain**—to display the other strike prices and months of options available for this stock.

- **Research**—provides a display of fundamental and technical data for both the stock and this option.

- **Calculators**—allows you to calculate the returns, which may include commissions or other costs and access to a Black-Scholes model for calculating the theoretical value of an option.

- **Search by Symbol**—allows you to view the risk-reward for the other strike price combinations on that stock for the different expiration months.

- **Add to Portfolio**—allows easy insertion of the information to track your stock and option position over time until expiration of the option.

- **Profit/Loss Chart**—a graphic of the option and stock price on a profit/loss chart.

The More Info key is a convenient and time-saving link to other sites or pages for information relative to that company. By taking advantage of the power of the internet for access to many financial sites, PowerOptions is your options portal to provide most of the information you might need to compare and analyze the protective strategies that match your risk-reward tolerance.

Some Cautions

This may sound too easy to be true. And usually when things look too easy or optimistic, there are traps waiting to catch you. That is the case here also. There are many things that can go wrong. At any time, a company might have a negative earnings surprise, an early earnings warning announcement or some other unforeseen market event that was previously mentioned. You may also find yourself in a rampant downward market where most positions in your portfolio will show a steady decline. In May of 2008, one of the co-authors of this text wanted to look for a covered call position. Instead of using his normal criteria, he decided to screen for large cap stocks that were in an uptrend but under $25.00 per share, and still offered a reasonable return. Seven potential trades matched the criteria and he selected OfficeMax (OMX).

Covered Call on Large Cap Stock: May 19th, 2008

Buy 200 shares of OMX at $20.43 ($4,086 total investment)
Sell to Open 2 June 20 calls at $1.05 ($210 income generated)
Total Cost / Break Even (not including commissions) = $19.38
Maximum Return = $0.62 per share (3.2 percent return on investment)

The hope was that OMX would remain above $20.00 per share and the covered call would be assigned. On June 12th, about 8 days from expiration, OMX had fallen to roughly $18.15 per share, which was $1.23 below the initial break-even. Conventional covered call techniques would recommend rolling down the call. He could buy to close the June call and sell to open a July 17.5 call to limit the loss. But, he tried something different. On June 19th (one day before June expiration), OMX had fallen to $17.18. He bought to close the June 20 calls for $0.05, sold to open the July 17.5 calls for $0.65, and at the same time purchased in-the-money 2009 January 20 strike puts at $4.20 per contract.

Rolled Position: June 19th, 2008

Buy to Close 2 June 20 calls at $0.05 ($10)
New Position Cost Basis = $19.43
Sell to Open 2 July 17.5 calls at $0.65
Buy to Open 2 January 2009 20 strike puts at $4.20
New Position Cost Basis = $22.98

He would freely admit that this was a ridiculous roll out position. Seven months of protection had been purchased, but the sold call was well below the cost basis. If the position was assigned at $17.50, at July expiration, a significant loss would be realized. He did not have to worry about assignment as OMX continued down, and down, and down. Approaching July expiration, OMX had dropped to a low of $10.89 per share on July 15th. The July call options were essentially worthless, but the protective puts had a value of $9.90. The position could be liquidated at this time for a value of $20.79 with a loss of $2.19 per share (9.5 percent loss on the position). So the trade was a loss; what is our point?

In a two-month time period, shares of OMX dropped 47 percent. A 47 percent decline in two months! Simply rolling the covered calls would have reduced the loss to about 40 percent. By purchasing the protective put, the loss on the position was limited to 9.5 percent of the capital that was invested. And there is still 5 months protection in place to continue to manage the position, generate income, and lower the unrealized loss. For privacy's sake we won't mention which author entered this trade.

The OMX trade reinforces some of the most important investment ideas.

1. First, even though everything looks right and matches the criteria you think will work, there are no guarantees in the market. At the time that the trade was entered, OMX was trading above its 50 day moving average, was a large cap stock, had a good broker recommendation and a good average volume. But still the stock fell.

2. Second, you have to be prepared and plan for the unexpected. During this two-month decline, there were no early earnings warning announcements or negative news from OMX, it just fell in price with the rest of the market during a time of concern for retail stores. The biggest one-day decline for OMX during this two-month period was on July 8th when Office Depot warned that its same store sales would be down 10 percent for the upcoming quarter. This dragged shares of OMX down about 11 percent, even though OMX had not released any news or guidance. Other competitors such as Staples also declined due to the news from Office Depot.

3. Third, management techniques are essential in any options trade. You cannot simply enter into a trade and expect that everything will work out the way you planned. If we had just purchased OMX and let it ride, thinking that eventually it would come back in price, we might have an unrealized loss of nearly 50 percent. Hindsight is always 20-20, however. Would it have been better to purchase the 20 strike put as the co-author

did and then sell the stock at $17.18? Yes, the loss on the stock would have been greatly reduced and the put option would have a gain of over 50 percent. At the time the management position was entered, he felt the stock would move back up in price.

4. Finally, even with a 9.5 percent unrealized loss, do you think he is happy that he purchased the 2009 January 20 strike put when he did? Well, he is not dancing in the streets because of it, but yes, he is happy he purchased the protection when he did. It would have cost more not having the insurance in place. Why did he hold on to the position for this long without trying to exit when the position had an 8 percent loss or less? Refer back to Chapter 2 and the section regarding the "human element" of investing. He was not wrong on this stock, he was just early—at least that is what he mutters to himself around the halls of the office.

Back Testing

One last thing to consider in your search for the best stocks by using a screening program is the ability to back test your screening parameters. Some parameters are more important than others. If you can back test those parameters, you have the possibility of really improving your investment results. Back testing can provide that extra level of confidence in the selection of parameters that you are using for stock and option selection. It allows the user to test the validity of a screening process by applying the screening parameters to a historical set of data representative of the market conditions in the past. Depending on what parameter values are chosen, different stocks would match your protective strategy criteria. Back testing is another means to increase your probability of success.

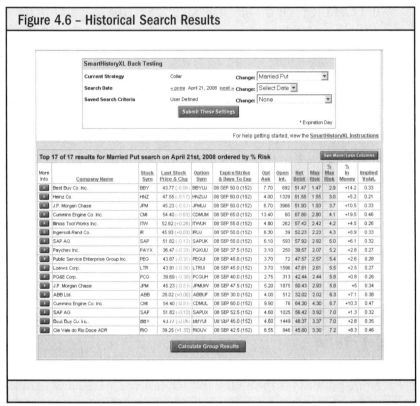

Figure 4.6 – Historical Search Results

SmartHistoryXL Back Testing

		Change:	
Current Strategy	Collar	Change:	Married Put
Search Date	« prev April 21, 2008 next »	Change:	Select Date
Saved Search Criteria	User Defined	Change:	None

Submit These Settings

* Expiration Day

For help getting started, view the SmartHistoryXL Instructions

Top 17 of 17 results for Married Put search on April 21st, 2008 ordered by % Risk

See More/Less Columns

More Info	Company Name	Stock Sym	Last Stock Price & Chg	Option Sym	Expire/Strike & Days To Exp	Opt Ask	Open Int.	Net Debit	Max Risk	% Max Risk	% In Money	Implied Volat.
	Best Buy Co. Inc.	BBY	43.77 (-0.06)	BBYUJ	08 SEP 50.0 (152)	7.70	692	51.47	1.47	2.9	+14.2	0.33
	Heinz Co.	HNZ	47.55 (-0.17)	HNZUJ	08 SEP 50.0 (152)	4.00	1329	51.55	1.55	3.0	+5.2	0.21
	J.P. Morgan Chase	JPM	45.23 (-0.53)	JPMUJ	08 SEP 50.0 (152)	6.70	3966	51.93	1.93	3.7	+10.5	0.33
	Cummins Engine Co. Inc.	CMI	54.40 (-0.83)	CDMUM	08 SEP 65.0 (152)	13.40	60	67.80	2.80	4.1	+19.5	0.46
	Illinois Tool Works Inc.	ITW	52.62 (+0.26)	ITWUK	08 SEP 55.0 (152)	4.80	262	57.42	2.42	4.2	+4.5	0.26
	Ingersoll-Rand Co.	IR	45.93 (+0.03)	IRUJ	08 SEP 50.0 (152)	6.30	39	52.23	2.23	4.3	+8.9	0.33
	SAP AG	SAP	51.82 (-0.13)	SAPUK	08 SEP 55.0 (152)	6.10	593	57.92	2.92	5.0	+6.1	0.32
	Paychex Inc.	PAYX	36.47 (-0.23)	PQXUU	08 SEP 37.5 (152)	3.10	250	39.57	2.07	5.2	+2.8	0.27
	Public Service Enterprise Group Inc.	PEG	43.87 (-0.31)	PEGUI	08 SEP 45.0 (152)	3.70	72	47.57	2.57	5.4	+2.6	0.28
	Loews Corp.	LTR	43.91 (-0.36)	LTRUI	08 SEP 45.0 (152)	3.70	1596	47.61	2.61	5.5	+2.5	0.27
	PG&E Corp.	PCG	39.69 (-0.36)	PCGUH	08 SEP 40.0 (152)	2.75	313	42.44	2.44	5.8	+0.8	0.26
	J.P. Morgan Chase	JPM	45.23 (-0.53)	JPMUW	08 SEP 47.5 (152)	5.20	1875	50.43	2.93	5.8	+5	0.34
	ABB Ltd.	ABB	28.02 (+0.05)	ABBUF	08 SEP 30.0 (152)	4.00	512	32.02	2.02	6.3	+7.1	0.38
	Cummins Engine Co. Inc.	CMI	54.40 (-0.83)	CDMUL	08 SEP 60.0 (152)	9.90	76	64.30	4.30	6.7	+10.3	0.47
	SAP AG	SAP	51.82 (-0.13)	SAPUX	08 SEP 52.5 (152)	4.60	1025	56.42	3.92	7.0	+1.3	0.32
	Best Buy Co. Inc.	BBY	43.77 (-0.06)	BBYUI	08 SEP 45.0 (152)	4.60	1449	48.37	3.37	7.0	+2.8	0.35
	Cia Vale do Rio Doce ADR	RIO	39.25 (+1.32)	RIOUV	08 SEP 42.5 (152)	6.55	846	45.80	3.30	7.2	+8.3	0.46

Calculate Group Results

Source: PowerOptions (www.poweropt.com)

For this example, we used the same criteria used in the sample screen in Figure 4.4 and looked for positions that would have fit these criteria on April 21, 2008 (roughly three months back in time). To further restrict the number of results, we adjusted the expiration time frame to only show put options that had 150 days to 180 days (5 to 6 months) to expiration and for the stocks to only be between $25.00 and $55.00 per share.

There were 17 results that matched the search criteria on April 21, 2008. That is all well and good, but what does it mean? We need to further analyze the results to see how they fared in the next few

Figure 4.7 – Summary of Historical Search Results

▶	☐	Best Buy Co. Inc.	BBY	43.77	08 SEP 45	BBYUI	4.60	48.37
▶	☐	Cia Vale do Rio Doce ADR	RIO	39.25	08 SEP 42.5	RIOUV	6.55	45.80

Remove all checked results [Remove]

Summary

 # Successful positions: 3 out of 17 (18%)
Avg. % Return: -1.9%
QQQQ % Return: -4.0% (4/21/2008 to 7/17/2008)
SPX % Return: -11.4% (4/21/2008 to 7/17/2008)

Source: PowerOptions (www.poweropt.com)

months or at the respective expiration date. In order to achieve this, you would simply click the "Calculate Group Results" button at the bottom of the screen. This shows the gain or loss from each position up to today's date. The most important feature of the Group Results is the "Summary" section for all trades.

These results show that every position is not coming out smelling like roses. Only 3 out of the 17 potential married put positions are showing a profit so far. But, with only an 18 percent success rate, the average loss for the 17 married put positions is only -1.9 percent. During the same time period, the broader based market indicators such as QQQQ and the S&P 500 Index (SPX) had fallen -4.0 percent and -11.4 percent, respectively. It is very unlikely that any investor would have traded all 17 positions that matched the criteria on April 21st, but this does illustrate the advantage of using protective strategies. Another important point about the summary in this example is that the limited loss on the positions does not include any management or adjustment techniques. These techniques could have been applied to several of the 17 positions over the last three months. Even without the management techniques applied, the married put positions still had a much lower loss than the listed market indicators. We use the protective strategies to limit our losses and preserve the invested capital. This summary shows that would have been achieved even in a down market during this recent time frame.

REVIEW

Married puts and collar spread trades are neutral to bullish investment strategies. Even though these strategies offer fantastic protection, you still want to look for stocks that have good fundamental and technical indicators. But even if you find a stock that has good bullish signals, there is no guarantee that the stock will move in the desired direction. This is one of the main reasons why you should be trading these protective strategies. You always need to be prepared for the unexpected and be ready to adjust your position in case of an adverse stock movement. You could spend hours looking through newspapers, looking at individual stock charts or researching individual stock listings, but a faster and more efficient way to identify potential stocks for these strategies is to use the patented SmartSearchXL tool on PowerOptions. This tool will help you quickly find only those stocks that match your desired fundamental and technical indicators.

Chapter 5

SELECTING THE PROPER PROTECTIVE COMBINATION

In Chapter 3, we outlined in detail the numerous protective combinations an investor can use to protect their positions. Each investor will have a different risk-reward tolerance. Utilizing these protective strategies allows you to create combinations where you can be protected while at the same time be slightly aggressive. The concept behind these protective strategies is to limit the maximum risk on the position while attempting to lower the daily cost of insurance.

In Chapter 4, we described some of the criteria you can use to identify neutral to bullish stocks. This allowed us to introduce the patented SmartSearchXL tool available only from PowerOptions. This tool allows you to put in your specific criteria to find only those positions that match your expectations and requirements. In less than a second, only those results that match your restrictions will be displayed. As we noted, nothing is a guarantee. Even though a stock matched a bullish set of criteria, that does not mean the stock will move up in price (OfficeMax).

Even though we explained our recommended techniques for the protective strategies and the types of stocks we might look for when entering these positions, your personal risk-reward tolerance might differ from ours. We also realize that you may be using different tools or your own equations when evaluating a potential married put or collar spread strategy. In this chapter, we will outline the criteria you might use to set up most of the combinations described in Chapter 3 using the SmartSearchXL tool as our guide. Most of the discussion in this chapter will be centered on our recommended married put and collar spread strategies; we will also discuss the stock's volatility, implied volatility and the delta.

Trading Tip: Using the Greeks

If you are an experienced options investor, you might be wondering why we have yet to mention any specifics regarding the Greeks: Delta, Theta, Gamma, Vega, and Rho. You may also be curious why we have not gone into any depth regarding stock volatility or the options' implied volatility. Using the patented search tools on PowerOptions, you can screen by most of those criteria, and those you cannot screen by you will be able to view with a simple click of your mouse. Believe it or not, these types of criteria are not important when you are screening for either of these protective strategies. When trading the protective strategies, you should spend more time focusing on the stock criteria previously discussed; the maximum risk and the potential return on the investment.

CRITERIA FOR FINDING THE RIGHT STOCKS

We have already discussed some of the criteria you might consider using to identify a neutral to bullish stock in the last chapter. These suggestions were:

- Percent EPSG greater than 7 percent
- Price/Earnings Ratio between 0 to 70
- Broker Recommendation less than 2.6
- Percent Dividend Yield greater than 0
- Market Capitalization greater than 1 billion
- Average Stock Volume greater than 300,00 per day
- Stocks greater than the 50 day moving average
- Stock price between $9.00 and $200.00

These are just some general criteria that help identify uptrending stocks with a few fundamental criteria. There are a variety of criteria that you can use in the SmartSearchXL tool to help you find only those stocks that match your requirements.

In this chapter, we want to discuss the criteria and guidelines you should look for to identify the protective combinations that are best suited for your risk-reward tolerance.

The standard married put trade is simple to identify. Once you have found a stock or a group of stocks that match your fundamental and technical criteria, you can simply go to an option chain at your broker and select the next month out, out-of-the-money put option. To calculate the maximum risk, add the price of the stock to the put option premium and then subtract the strike price of the put option.

Married Put Maximum Risk =
(Stock Price + Put Ask Price) – Put Strike Price

(For the example in Chapter 1, this would be $50.00 + $0.50 - $45.00 = $5.50)

Most standard married put trades still have a relatively high risk and a short time frame in which to make a profit. Depending on the stock, the maximum risk for the standard married put trade might be as high as 25 percent if the option premium is high due to volatility. Analyzing the individual stocks, looking up the potential options on a chain, and then doing the equations by hand can be very time consuming. If you feel compelled to trade the standard married put positions in which you purchase a near month, out-of-the-money put option, the SmartSearchXL tool will save you valuable research and analysis time.

Figure 5.1 shows the PowerOptions default criteria for the more conservative in-the-money, far out in time married put positions. As you can see from the figure, this tool allows you to screen for a wide variety of stock and option criteria. To identify the suggested married put positions, you would want to focus on the Option Expiration Time Frame and Days to Expiration fields (located on the left), the range in-the-money or out-of-the-money (also on the far left), the Max Risk (monetary risk) and % Max Risk. For a standard married put position you can simply set the Option Expiration Time Frame to the next available month, or select "All Months" but limit the Days to Expiration to be no greater than 45 days out in time. You would also need to adjust the range from in-the-money to out-of-the-money. Lastly, you would have to adjust the % Maximum Risk range, as most standard married puts would have a maximum risk higher than 10 percent. But, if you were looking for near term, out-of-the-money

Figure 5.1 – The SmartSearchXL Married Put Parameter Field

	Greater Than	Less Than		Greater Than	Less Than
Search Settings Saved As:	Married Put Book		Save	Delete	Submit These Settings

Description: Search for Chapter 4 with low IV

Sort Results Table By: % Risk

Option Expiration Time Frame: All Months

Days To Expiration: 150 to 700

○ Order results HIGHEST to LOWEST
◉ Order results LOWEST to HIGHEST

Show in-the-money
Strikes [ ] to [ ]
% in money [ ] to 20

Show out-of-the-money
Strikes [ ] to [ ]
% out money [ ] to [ ]

Earnings Date
☐ Between now and expiration.
☐ Not between now and expiration.

Ex Dividend Date
☐ Between now and expiration.
☐ Not between now and expiration

Search by Symbol
Stock Symbol: [ ]

	Greater Than	Less Than
Net Debit		to
Max Risk		to
% Risk	2.5	to 9
Option Volume Today	0	to
% Current Option Volume		to
Prev Option Volume		to
% Prev Option Volume		to
Open Interest	0	to
Stock Price	9	to 200
Stock Change Today		to
% Stock Change Today		to
Option Ask Price		to
Black-Scholes Ratio (50 Day)		to
Black-Scholes Ratio (SIV)		to
Delta		to
Implied Volatility		to
% Imp Volat Range		to
Volatility Ratio		to
% To Double		to
Put/Call Vol. Ratio		to
Ask Time Value		to
Ask % Time Value		to
Bid/Ask Spread		to

	Greater Than	Less Than
% EPS Growth	7	to
Price/Earnings	0	to 70
Price/Earnings/Growth		to
% Of 52 Week Range		to
Average Broker Rec		to 2.6
Average Rec Change		to
% Stock Volume		to
Shares Outstanding		to
% Dividend Yield	0	to
Beta		to
Historical Volatility		to
Market Capitalization	10000	to
Price/Sales		to
Average Stock Volume	300	to
% Probability Above		to
Put/Call OI Ratio		to
Z Score		to
Z" Score		to
Springate		to
RSI		to
% BB (20)		to
% Band Width (20)		to

Sectors/Industries: All Sectors/Industries

Recommended Lists (Create/Modify Lists): No Lists

Simple Moving Average: Stock Price > SMA50

Source: PowerOptions (www.poweropt.com)

puts with a potentially lower risk, this powerful tool will find those opportunities for you in less than a second—if they are available.

RECOMMENDED MARRIED PUT CRITERIA

You can start by using the default criteria shown above as a stepping-stone to create your own personal search. In Chapter 3 we outlined the slight differences in maximum risk and break even points for a 6 month out and a 12 month out position. Depending on the expiration cycle of the stock that was detailed in Chapter 1, an optionable stock might not have an option series that is 6 months (180 days out) or 12 months (365 days out). To solve this problem, the default Option Expiration Time Frame is screening against "All Months" but the Days to Expiration has been limited to 150 days (approximately 5 months) to 700 days (approximately 2 years).

The 6 month and 12 month examples from Chapter 3 were shown for simplicity. When you are screening for potential married puts, it is a good idea to screen using a wide range of expiration months to include the different option series. You may find married put positions on good stocks with a put option that is 8 or 18 months out in time. These are still viable trades and should not be excluded from your search results.

The next criterion we want to focus on is the percent in-the-money range. This allows us to limit how deep in-the-money the put option is from the stock price. Earlier we discussed that if the put option is too deep in-the-money, the risk might be very low, but the stock will need to have a very significant gain before a profit can be realized or a reasonable management technique can be applied. We suggest limiting your selections to the put options that are less than 20 percent in-the-money. As previously mentioned, the average tendency is for the market to gain 10 percent per year. Expecting a stock to gain 30 percent or 40 percent on average is unrealistic, so it is best to limit how far the put is in-the-money. Notice that there is no value in the greater than box for percent in-the-money. If you wished to screen for put options that were at least 5 percent in-the-money you would simply add a "5" into the first field for the "percent in money" field.

The next default criterion is the "percent risk." This allows you to limit the percent maximum risk that you feel you can tolerate on a married put position. The default settings are looking for only those married put trades that have a maximum risk greater than 2.5 percent but less than 9 percent. You may be curious why we limited the lower range of the percent maximum risk. The goal of these positions is to limit the loss as much as possible, so why limit the positions that have a 1 percent or 2 percent risk? Our experience with married puts has shown that positions with less than a 2 percent risk are too deep in-the-money. The protection is great, we cannot argue that, but the option most likely would be greater than 20 percent in-the-money (note how these two criteria relate to one another). A much larger movement would be required to reach the break even point or manage the position.

That being said, this simply illustrates the power of the patented SmartSearchXL tool. If you wanted to screen for married puts that offered a percent maximum risk as low as 2 percent, 1 percent, or less you can simply adjust the criteria to match your tolerance. The system will find only those trades that match your desired risk level.

In our opinion, these are the three most important option criteria to use when identifying a married put position. You want to look for put options that are at least 150 days to 700 days out in time. This will lower your daily cost of insurance while also giving you plenty of time to manage the position and generate income to help lower the cost basis. You want to limit how far in-the-money the put option is so that you are not expecting an unrealistic gain in the underlying stock. Finally, the name of the game is limiting your risk and preserving your capital. You want to set the percent maximum risk to a level that matches your personal tolerance. If you wanted to look for a position with a percent maximum risk less than 2 percent or less than 1 percent, simply adjust the filter. However, if you lower the risk, you may need to increase the limitation of the percent in-the-money range. You may not find any married puts that have less than a 1 percent maximum risk but are also less than 20 percent in-the-money. Positions with that low of a risk may be as high as 30 percent in-the-money or more. Even if you choose to manually find these trades and not benefit from the SmartSearchXL tool, we suggest that you focus on these criteria first when researching and analyzing your positions.

Does this mean that you should only use these three criteria when filtering for married put trades? Absolutely not! The SmartSearchXL tool has over 20 different option related criteria you can use. Let's take a quick look at the other criteria you can use and how they relate to the married put trade.

Liquidity Criteria

The co-authors of this book highly recommend trading options that have a high option volume and open interest in most strategies. For the married put trade we have to make some adjustments to our usual requirements. In Figure 5.1 you can see that the default criteria are looking for a minimum Option Volume Today greater than zero (at least one contract traded today) and a minimum Open Interest of greater than zero (at least one contract opened over the life of the option). These criteria measure the liquidity of the option or the amount of trading activity for the option. If you were trading covered calls or naked puts, we would suggest looking for a much higher volume or open interest. Most options volume and activity happen with the near term options that are one or two months out in time. Since we are looking for options that are at least five months out in time, we cannot expect a lot of daily activity. If you prefer only to trade options that have a certain volume on the day you are placing the trade or you look for a minimum open interest, simply change the settings to match your requirements.

As you can see, there are also criteria for Previous Option Volume (the total contracts traded the previous trading day) and Percent Current and Percent Previous Option Volume. The percent option volume fields allow you to screen for stocks that have had an increase in total option compared to the average volume of the last 30 days. These are useful for more aggressive strategies such as long calls or puts and long straddle positions, but they do not really factor in to the protection calculations of a married put position.

Other Risk and Cost Criteria

The first two option criteria in the center section of Figure 5.1 are Net Debit and Max. Risk. The net debit is the total cost of the position, including both the cost of the stock and the ask price of the protective put. This has already been limited somewhat by the stock price limitation of $9.00 to $200.00. If you were only planning to buy 100 shares of stock and had $5,000 available to invest, you could limit the stock price to less than $50.00, but you would need to account for the price of the put. The net debit field would allow you to limit the total cost of the position to less than $50.00 per share, which would include both the stock price plus the cost of the put.

The Max. Risk (maximum risk) allows you to filter by the total monetary risk for the position. We like to use the percentage rather than the monetary maximum risk, but that is just personal preference. If you wanted to make sure that you were risking less than $2.00 per share regardless of the percentage, you could easily add that into the criteria.

The SmartSearchXL tool will also allow you to limit the total cost of the option (Ask Price), the monetary time value (Ask Time Value) or the percentage time value (Ask Percent Time Value). The net debit can be used to limit the total cost of the position, but you could also limit the cost of the put option. The percent time value is roughly the same as the percent maximum risk that was already discussed. The time value is your total risk when you purchase in-the-money put options for protection.

Another cost criterion that is commonly used is the Bid/Ask Spread. You can use this criterion to look for put options that have a smaller bid/ask spread. If you only wanted to find put options where the ask price was no more than $0.50 greater than the bid price, simply enter that value into the 'Less Then' field. Far out in time options tend to have a wide bid/ask spread, partly due to the lack of volume or activity. You should not be surprised to find married put positions that are 12 months out in time and have a bid/ask spread as high as $2.00 or more. You may feel that this spread is too wide for your preference, but a high bid/ask spread also has an advantage. The maximum risk and percent maximum risk values shown are calculated using the listed ask price for the put option. If you have a wide bid/ask spread, you may be able to place a limit order and purchase the put at a slightly lower cost. This will decrease the maximum risk for the position.

Delta and Implied Volatility Criteria

The delta measures the movement of the put option in relation to a one-point movement of the stock price. As explained in Chapter

1, put options have a negative delta as the price changes inversely to the stock (If the stock goes up, the put decreases in total value. If the stock falls, the put increases in total value). An at-the-money put option will typically have a delta of -0.5. If the stock moves up $1.00 in value, we would expect the put option to drop -$0.50 in price. If the stock dropped $1.00, we would expect to gain $0.50 on our put option. Put options that are deeper in-the-money will have a delta closer to -1 and deep out-of-the-money put options will have a delta closer to zero.

The first default criteria that were discussed already help limit the delta range of the potential trades. By limiting the put options to be less than 20 percent out-of-the-money and looking for a limited maximum risk of 2.5 to 9 percent, we typically find only those options that are at least 1 strike in-the-money but less than 4 strikes in-the-money. The general delta range of those options is typically between -0.6 and -0.8. In this strategy we want to focus more on the total maximum risk for the position rather than the specific movement of the put option in relation to the stock price. If you wanted to find deeper in-the-money put options that inversely tracked the stock closer to a 1:1 ratio, simply enter in a filter for delta of less than -0.9 (puts have a negative delta but number order is still a constant, -1 is less than -0.9).

Implied volatility is commonly referred to as the measure of future risk for the option. Options with a higher implied volatility are usually a sign that some event might be coming up that could cause the stock to fluctuate in price. Options with a higher implied volatility also tend to have larger premiums, as there is more potential risk in buying or selling the option due to the speculation of the upcoming event. Selling options with a higher volatility means you can collect an inflated premium, but you are also taking on extra risk because the stock might fluctuate in price against the position. Buying options with a lower implied volatility means you are purchasing a potentially deflated option, but you may not see a lot of movement in the stock that would hurt your chances for a profit.

Over the years, the co-authors of this book have developed a certain sentiment regarding implied volatility. Our sentiment is that implied volatility is the most talked about, misunderstood and thus, the most commonly misused criteria by many options investors. The great thing about the married put strategy is that the maximum risk is locked in. If the implied volatility of the put option increases or decreases, the liquidation value of the position might shift, but you still have the right to exercise the put option and sell the shares of stock at the strike price at any time. This may result in a loss, but the loss would never be greater than the initial maximum risk.

Another reason why we are not focusing too much on implied volatility in this strategy is that far out options typically have a relatively low implied volatility. Near term options that are less than three months out in time are more sensitive to changes in implied volatility caused by speculation or fluctuation in the stock price. Options that are six months or more out in time are less subject to the near term changes, although a severe decrease or increase in the stock price would affect the implied volatilities of all expiration months.

THE KISS RULE

"Keep it Simple Simple!" Yes, there are other variations of the KISS rule, but we prefer this version, as it doubly emphasizes the "Simple." Another variation we like is "Keep it Simple to Start!" Although there are various criteria available in the SmartSearchXL tool, and there are multitudes of other criteria that you could use to analyze a married put position, you do not want to be too restrictive. When you are looking for a good married put candidate, first identify the stocks that you think are strong, stocks that you would not mind holding in your account for several months at a time. Then look for protective puts that are at least 5 months out in time, are less than 20 percent in-the-money and that have a percent maximum risk less than 9 percent. You may have tools to help you identify certain stocks and you could then look up the options individually and do all the calculations by hand, but that is extremely time consuming.

The SmartSearchXL tool will allow you to do all of that research at once. Start with the basics, screening for stocks that match the general criteria outlined in Chapter 4 with the three option criteria just mentioned. If you feel there are too many results, simply adjust the other criteria that match your personal preferences and run the search again. In less than a second, the SmartSearchXL tool will find only those positions that match your desired risk threshold. As shown in Chapter 4, you can then access the More Information button to quickly research more details on the stock or the option. This tool will greatly reduce your research time and is of great value in the decision making process.

CRITERIA FOR FINDING THE RECOMMENDED COLLAR SPREAD TRADE

Just like the standard married put, the standard collar spread is easy to identify. You can simply find a stock that you like, identify the near term, out-of-the-money put option that matches your risk tolerance, then find the near term, out-of-the-money call option that will pay for the cost of the put but is still within a reasonable range to potentially be assigned. Standard collar spreads can offer a good return and somewhat limit risk if the market is fairly bullish. Just like the standard married put trade, the near term, standard collar is essentially a hit or miss trade. You can drastically reduce the overall risk and have more time to profit on the position by purchasing a far out, in-the-money put. Selling an out-of-the-money, near term call option will lower the initial cost basis and generate income. Selling near term calls will also increase your annualized income over selling a further out call option.

Figure 5.2 is very similar to Figure 5.1, but there are some subtle differences. Applying the KISS rule, we do not need to spend too much time in this section. The default criteria, which is our suggested starting point, is the same stock criteria as the default married put search just discussed. The protective put criteria are also the same. This search is looking for put options that are between 150 to 700 days out in time and less than 20 percent in-the-money. The maximum risk and percentage maximum risk for the position are also similar, as we are looking for long-term debit collar spreads that have less than 10 percent total risk. The only difference in the collar risk calculations is the addition of the call premium that was received, which lowered the cost basis of the spread. We will not spend time covering the wide range of other filters such as call delta or implied volatility in this section. For more information about those filters, see the discussion in the previous section. All of the filters are available to use just as they were in the married put screen, but we want to "Keep it Simple to Start" here.

First, notice in Figure 5.2 that there are now two selection fields for Option Expiration Time Frame and Days to Expiration, one for the

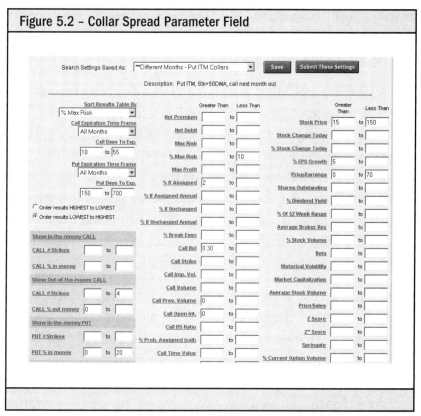

Figure 5.2 – Collar Spread Parameter Field

Source: PowerOptions (www.poweropt.com)

call option and one for the put option. The put option settings have remained the same, but the call option's days to expiration are limited to 10 to 55 days out in time. You want to look for call options that are near term expiration to maximize the annual income that is generated. The near term call option will not pay for the time value for the put option, but the premium will reduce the initial cost basis.

Second, there are now also two sections for screening the range in-the-money or out-of-the-money. The default criteria is screening for near term call options that are less than four strikes out-of-the-money and at least zero percent out-of-the-money. The out-of-the-money strike range is limited to less than four strikes as the deep out-of-the-money call premiums are too low.

Third, there is a small field just beneath the put option in-the-money or out-of-the-money fields that is not shown in Figure 5.2. This field will allow you to set the screen to look for collars where the call strike is greater than the put strike. This is important because if the call strike is lower than the put option and the shares are assigned in the first month, a loss might be realized. There are positions where this technique might yield a small profit in the first month, but they are rare. It is recommended that the call strike is greater than the put strike price in a long-term debit collar spread.

In the center section of the parameter field there is a net debit field, but there is also a Net Premium field. The net premium is the difference between the two option premiums, calculated as Call Bid Price minus Put Ask Price. It is unlikely that the premium received from selling the near term call will cover the cost of the protective put. The results for this strategy will have a negative premium. You could easily limit the range of net premium to match your personal preference, but the premium is already factored into the percent maximum risk for the spread.

The major different criteria in the collar spread screen are the Percent if Assigned, Percent if Unchanged and the Percent Probability Above the Call Strike Price. Once a call is sold, turning a married put position into a collar spread, the maximum return is capped. A return if assigned at the strike price can be calculated, as can a percent return if the stock is unchanged, or remains at the same price through the call expiration date. A return cannot be calculated in a married put position because the potential profits are unlimited.

The percent if assigned is the maximum return for the collar spread if the call is assigned at near term expiration. This return takes into account the appreciation on the stock and the remaining theoretical value of the put option.

Percent if Assigned = (Strike Price – Initial Net Debit)
+ Theoretical Put Value

Initial Net Debit

The theoretical value of the put option is calculated using the Black-Scholes pricing model. The Black-Scholes model takes into account five factors to estimate the theoretical price of the option: stock price, strike price of the option, days remaining to expiration, interest rate, and the volatility of the stock. For the collar spread equations, the strike price of the sold call is used as the stock price in the equation. The theoretical value shows what the put option might be worth if the stock was trading right at the short call strike price at the near term expiration. Even if the shares are assigned, the protective put could still be sold for some remaining value, thus increasing the potential return.

The default criteria are looking for only those collar spreads that have at least a 2 percent return if assigned. You want to make sure that if you are assigned in the first month, then the position would still be profitable.

Similar to the percent return if assigned is the percent return if unchanged. The percent return if unchanged reflects the potential return on the collar spread if the stock remains at the same price between now and the short-term expiration date. This return calculation also uses the Black-Scholes pricing model to calculate the remaining, theoretical price of the option. In this case, the current price of the stock is used for the stock price since it is assumed that the stock price did not change in the first month.

$$\text{Percent if Unchanged} = \frac{(\text{Current Stock Price} - \text{Initial Net Debit}) + \text{Theoretical Put Value}}{\text{Initial Net Debit}}$$

There is not a filter for the percent if unchanged set in the default criteria, but this filter can help you limit the number of results. One suggestion is to look for debit collar spreads that offer a theoretical percent if unchanged greater than zero. If the stock remains at the same price, it is possible that the put option will not have lost a lot of value. The call option would expire worthless and the stock and put option could be sold for no loss or a slight gain. A better tactic would be to hold the position and sell another call against the married put position.

The last additional criterion that is important to the long-term debit collar spread is the Percent Probability Above. This is the theoretical

---

Trading Tip: Be Cautious with Theoretical Pricing

The Black-Scholes pricing model has limitations when calculating prices for far out options. In addition, the calculated theoretical price is not set in stone. Many factors can cause an option to be priced higher or lower if the stock is at a certain price on a certain date out in time. It helps to screen for collar spreads that would offer a positive return if assigned, but the actual return might be slightly lower depending on the price of the put option at expiration. That being said, you really want to include the remaining price of the put option when comparing potential collar spread positions.

probability that the stock will be trading above the call strike price at near term expiration. In simple terms, the probability shows the likelihood that the stock will be trading at or above the call strike price at expiration, based on the past trading range and volatility of the underlying stock. An at-the-money call option will typically have a 50 percent probability. There is a 50-50 chance that the stock will be trading above its current price or below its current price in a 30 day time period. Call options that are deeper out-of-the-money will have a lower probability of being assigned. In this strategy, the sold call will be at least two strikes out-of-the-money or more. You should not expect to have a probability greater than 50 percent, but you can use this parameter to limit the results.

Using the probability above in conjunction with the percent if assigned is a great way to search for trades that have a better probability of being assigned for a potential profit, while still limiting your maximum risk to 10 percent or less. You could run a search for collar spreads that have greater than 40 percent probability above, offer a potential return of greater than 2 percent, and where the maximum risk is less than 7 percent. You may not get many results, but you have potential for a decent return with a very limited risk in a one-month time frame. If the collar spread is not assigned, you still have an extended time period in which to continue generating income and lower the cost basis of the initial trade. As with the married put criteria, you can adjust the settings any way you want to match your desired profit requirement with your desired limited risk. We feel that the criteria that we mentioned are the best way to apply the KISS rule when screening for the long-term debit collar spreads. You can use the other various criteria to further limit your results and find the best position for your individual investing ideals. If you are using other tools to calculate these returns and probabilities by hand, we still feel that these are the criteria that you should focus on first.

SUGGESTIONS, RECOMMENDATIONS, BUT NO GUARANTEES

The default settings and the other criteria we outlined for these two strategies do not guarantee that you will profit on every position. In either the married put trade or the long-term debit collar, the stock needs to move up in price before a profit can be realized. The stock criteria that we used in both examples are looking for a good fundamental and technical base, but there are thousands of ways to screen for bullish stocks. We cannot guarantee that every stock that matches the criteria will rise in price in the first month or even over a one year time frame. Then again, no one else can guarantee that a stock will rise in price over a given time frame. If someone is bold enough to guarantee a rise in the stock price over a set period of time, they are either attempting to get you to purchase an extremely overpriced product or there are several strings attached.

That being said, we can guarantee that if you use these criteria as a guideline, you will not lose more than 9 percent on any married put trade or 10 percent on any long term debit collar spread. The maximum risk is locked in once the protective put is purchased. Even if the stock drops to $1.00 per share, you can still exercise the put and sell your shares at the put strike price. You will realize the maximum loss on the trade, but that limited loss is much better than having the stock drop to $1.00 with no protection in place.

USING MARRIED PUTS AND LONG TERM DEBIT COLLARS TO LOCK IN GAINS

What if you are not in the market to purchase new stock? You might be focusing your attention on several stocks in your portfolio that have gone up in price and have a very nice unrealized return. Now you have to question whether to sell the shares and take the profit or hold on to the shares and hope for a larger gain. The stock may continue to rise and you could sell for a larger profit, or the stock could fall, wiping out the previous unrealized gains. Or, consider this option: you could purchase a far out put option to protect most of the unrealized gains while still being in a position to further profit if the stock moves up in price.

This may be hard to believe considering the cost of a far out put option, but it is very possible and a very smart strategy to use. PowerOptions has simplified this process of protecting gains by creating the Position Insurance Tool.

Insurance Example

January 23rd, 2008 – Purchase Shares of APA (Apache Corp) at $85.00
Today's Price = $110.74
Total Unrealized Profit = $25.74
Total Unrealized Profit Percentage = 30.3 percent

You can now choose to sell the shares for a 30 percent gain or continue to hold on to the position if you think the stock will continue to rise. The risk with holding the stock is that there might be a swift decline and you would lose most of the unrealized return before you could react. The main equations you need to calculate the locked in profit when purchasing a far out put option are:

New Cost Basis = Original Cost Basis + Put Ask Price
Locked In Profit = Put Strike Price − New Cost Basis

You may also want to calculate the Put Percent Time Value, the Time Value per Month, and the Percent Locked in Profit. You could spend hours calculating these values by hand for all strikes in the various expiration months, or you can have it all done for you in a second with a few clicks.

To calculate the potential locked in profits, simply enter in the stock symbol, initial cost basis, and the expiration month during which

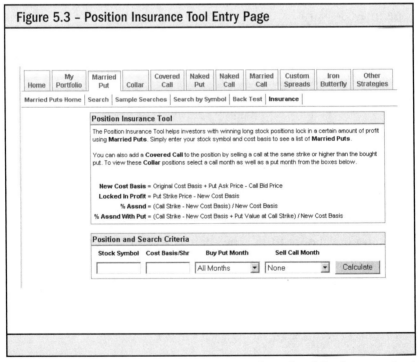

Figure 5.3 − Position Insurance Tool Entry Page

Source: PowerOptions (www.poweropt.com)

you might consider buying a put. For this example, the symbol APA was entered with a cost basis of $85.00. January 2009 was selected as the "Buy Put Month," assuming that the shares would be held for an additional 6 months to realize a larger profit if the stock continued up in price.

If APA were sold today, a profit of 30.3 percent would be realized. As the chart shows, there are many opportunities to purchase insurance and lock in profits for the position. The highest locked in profit is listed at the top of the results. You could purchase the 2009 January 125 strike put for $23.10. This would give you the right to sell shares of APA at $125.00 at any time between now and 2009 January expira-

Figure 5.4 - Married Put Locked In Protection

Position and Search Criteria

Stock Symbol	Cost Basis/Shr	Buy Put Month	Sell Call Month
APA	85	January 2009	None

Apache Corp. - Current Price: **$110.74** Current Profit: +25.74 (30.3%)

More Info	Put Symbol	Put Exp (Days)	Put Strike	Put Ask	Put Time Value	Put Time Value /Mo	New Cost Basis	Locked In Profit	% Locked In Profit
	APAMV	JAN 2009 (177)	125.00	$23.10	$8.84	$1.50	$108.10	$16.90	15.6%
	APAMU	JAN 2009 (177)	120.00	$19.80	$10.54	$1.79	$104.80	$15.20	14.5%
	APAMC	JAN 2009 (177)	115.00	$16.80	$12.54	$2.13	$101.80	$13.20	13.0%
	APAMB	JAN 2009 (177)	110.00	$14.10	$14.10	$2.39	$99.10	$10.90	11.0%
	APAMA	JAN 2009 (177)	105.00	$11.60	$11.60	$1.97	$96.60	$8.40	8.7%
	APAMT	JAN 2009 (177)	100.00	$9.40	$9.40	$1.59	$94.40	$5.60	5.9%
	APAMS	JAN 2009 (177)	95.00	$7.40	$7.40	$1.25	$92.40	$2.60	2.8%
	APAMR	JAN 2009 (177)	90.00	$5.80	$5.80	$0.98	$90.80	$-0.80	-0.9%
	APAMQ	JAN 2009 (177)	85.00	$4.30	$4.30	$0.73	$89.30	$-4.30	-4.8%

Source: PowerOptions (www.poweropt.com)

tion (177 days). Your new cost basis would be $108.10, with a locked in profit of $16.90.

You might be thinking: "But wait! APA is currently trading at $110.74. If the new cost basis is $108.10, that is only a $2.64 profit!" The new cost basis is $108.10, but you purchased the 125 strike put. You can sell to close shares of APA for $125 per share at any time. This would yield a profit of $16.90 per share, or 15.6 percent.

Why would you purchase a put option to lock in a 15.6 percent return when you could sell the shares today for a 30.3 percent return? You would want to purchase a put for insurance if you were planning on holding the stock in expectation of further gains in the stock price. If you hold the stock and it drops, you might give back most of the 30.3 percent return you had. If you lock in the profit now, you are guaranteed at least a 15.6 percent any time between now and the expiration date.

If you wished to add insurance to lock in profit but at the same time generate income, you can sell a call option against the new insurance position. You would need to calculate the percent if assigned and the percent if assigned including the remaining theoretical put price at near term expiration to compare the potential positions.

**Insurance Percent Assigned =
(Call Strike – New Cost Basis) / New Cost Basis**

**Insurance Percent Assigned With Put = (Call Strike – New Cost Basis
+ Put Value at Call Strike) / New Cost Basis**

Instead of doing these calculations for every strike price and every combination of long put and short call, you could simply select a month from the "Sell Call Month" field in the Position Insurance tool on PowerOptions and click "Calculate."

The call premium received changes the dynamic of the locked in profit and potential return. The first listed result now shows that the 2009 January 100 strike put could be purchased for $10.40 and the September 100 strike call could be sold for $13.00. This position insurance trade would have a locked in profit of $17.60, or 21.4 percent. If the call were assigned at expiration, the position would yield 21.4 percent.

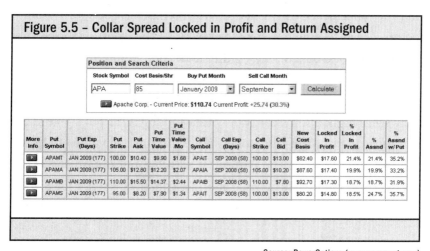

Figure 5.5 – Collar Spread Locked in Profit and Return Assigned

Source: PowerOptions (www.poweropt.com)

If you placed this position insurance collar spread and your shares of APA were assigned at 100, you could still sell to close the 100 strike put option that would still have 4 months of remaining time value. The estimated total return for this trade would be 35.2 percent; just about 5 percent higher than the current unrealized gains you have on APA.

ONE STOCK AT A TIME

If you own a stock that has not risen in price or you are getting ready to buy shares of a stock that you have been tracking, you should consider adding protection to those shares as well. You could simply pull up an option chain, look up the prices of each option and manually calculate all the risk calculations by hand to find the best protection—or you can use a tool that would do that for you.

Figure 5.6 illustrates a list of puts that can be purchased with the stock GMCR. The GMCR stock price is $42.07 and the put options listed have a strike price range of $25 to $55. All of the put options shown are for the month of December, about 7 months (197 days) out in time. This means the insurance we purchased is good for 7 months before it is necessary to renew the policy. In the column labeled "Net Debit," the total cost of buying the stock and buying the put for protection is shown. The December 55 put cost ($14.90) plus the stock price ($42.07) would have a net debit (cost) of $56.97. This total cost may seem high, but in reality, it is very modest. Our put strike at $55 is almost 13 points in-the-money. It has an inherent value of $13. We buy the stock for $42 and can sell it with the put option at $55. No matter how low the stock price goes, we can always sell it for $55 per share, with the purchase of the put option. To compare the maxi-

Figure 5.6 – PowerOptions Search By Symbol Tool

Green Mountain Coffee Roasters Inc. (GMCR) $ 42.07 (-1.00) -2.3 %

Stock Symbol: GMCR   Expiration Month: December   Filters: More Results   Submit   Lookup Symbol

More Info	Option Symb	Expire/Strike & Days To Exp	Opt Ask	Net Debit	Max Risk	% Max Risk	% Time Value	% In Money	Implied Volat.	Delta	% Prob. Above
	QGMXK	06 DEC 55.0 (197)	14.90	56.97	1.97	3.5	4.7	+30.73	0.47	-0.71	22.6
	QGMXJ	08 DEC 50.0 (197)	11.20	53.27	3.27	6.1	7.8	+18.85	0.48	-0.61	31.4
	QGMXI	08 DEC 45.0 (197)	7.90	49.97	4.97	9.9	11.8	+6.96	0.49	-0.49	42.5
	QGMXH	08 DEC 40.0 (197)	5.30	47.37	7.37	15.6	12.6	-4.92	0.51	-0.36	55.6
	QGMXG	08 DEC 35.0 (197)	3.40	45.47	10.47	23.0	8.1	-16.81	0.55	-0.24	69.6
	QGMXF	08 DEC 30.0 (197)	1.95	44.02	14.02	31.8	4.6	-28.69	0.57	-0.13	82.7
	QGMXE	08 DEC 25.0 (197)	1.00	43.07	18.07	42.0	2.4	-40.58	0.59	-0.05	92.7

Source: PowerOptions (www.poweropt.com)

mum risk and percentage risk of further out options, simply click the "Expiration Month" drop down menu.

REVIEW

These two strategies can be useful to any investor in many different ways. The married put positions guarantee a limited maximum risk on a long stock position. The criteria mentioned in this chapter are merely guidelines, suggested criteria that you should use as a stepping-stone to create your own positions that match your personal risk-reward tolerance. The long term debit collar spreads offer a limited maximum risk while at the same time generate monthly income into your account. You can use both of these strategies to lock in profits on a stock that has moved up that you are planning to hold for future gains. This allows you to still take advantage of the stock movement while guaranteeing a fair percentage of the unrealized gains on the stock position. The next step is to discuss some of the "dos and don'ts" when placing either a married put trade or collar spread trade with your broker.

Chapter 6

TIPS ON ENTERING THE PROTECTIVE STRATEGIES

You now have a general working knowledge of the protective strategies. We have explained why we feel you should be using these strategies in your portfolio. We have illustrated comparisons to the basic and more common options investment strategies and shown how the protective strategies will greatly reduce risk and exposure in your portfolio. We also discussed the advantages and disadvantages of potential married put or collar spread combinations to help you identify which setup might best match your personal risk-reward tolerance, provided you with some guidelines on the types of stocks you might want to look for in these strategies, and outlined the general options criteria you would use to identify the various strategy combinations.

In addition to that knowledge, we have shown you the capability of the powerful PowerOptions tools that will greatly reduce your research and analysis time when looking for these trades. Once you have found those positions that match your personal criteria, you are ready to place the trade with your broker. In this chapter we want to discuss some tips and rules of thumb when you are placing either a married put trade or a collar spread combination.

QUALIFICATION

To take advantage of the benefits of the protective strategies, you must first apply with your broker to trade options. We assume that most of you reading this text are already qualified to trade options at some level or another. For those of you who are just starting out in options investing, we will walk you through the general steps.

The first step is to review the information your broker should provide regarding their requirements and restrictions for options trading approval. These may include:

- Available funds or capital in your account
- Personal net worth
- Trading experience (number of stock trades per month or per year)
- Options trading experience (if you are applying for higher levels)

Every brokerage firm has their own requirements and restrictions on which strategies they will approve based on your trading experience and the type of trading account that you have. Most brokers will only allow a few option investment strategies to be traded in a retirement account, though more complex strategies might be allowed in a cash or margin account. Here is a general list of the different trading levels you can be approved for and the strategies that are allowed at each level.

- **Level I** – Buy stocks, mutual funds, short stock, trade covered calls.

- **Level II** – Buy calls, buy puts, trade covered puts
- **Level III** – Debit spreads, calendar call or put spreads, long straddles
- **Level IV** – Credit spreads, naked calls, and naked puts
- **Other Levels** – Some brokerage houses may have a higher level for selling naked calls, as they are a riskier strategy

Most major brokerage firms will allow you to buy puts and sell covered calls in almost every type of account, including retirement accounts. Your broker may require you to apply for Level I and Level II trading to be able to trade long puts and covered calls, but some may only require Level I approval. Being approved for these two levels is all you need in order to trade the married put or collar spread strategies.

Once you have identified the level of trading you will need and the requirements of your broker, the next step is to simply fill out the forms and apply. If you are not approved on your first attempt, contact your broker and try to find out any specifics as to why your application was not approved. If your broker feels that you do not have enough trading experience, place some more trades. You can enter into a few conservative trades in mutual funds or ETFs. After you have made several trades that you were comfortable with, simply reapply. If your broker says that they require a higher net worth, there is not much you may be able to do right now. You always have the choice to compare the requirements at other brokers and transfer your account if your current broker's requirements are too restrictive.

When you are approved to trade options, you will receive a pamphlet from the OCC (Options Clearing Corporation) called *Characteristics and Risks of Standardized Options*. It is important that you read the information in that pamphlet to become familiar with the different aspects of assignment and exercise as well as the industry's policies regarding options investing. You can quickly access this information and the most recent supplements any time at http://www.option-sclearing.com/publications/risks/riskchap1.jsp or http://www.cboe.com/Resources/Intro.aspx.

Now that you approved, you are ready to place your trade.

GENERAL TIPS

Advancements in internet and computer technology over the last 15 years have made trading securities a snap—or should we say, a click. Simply point and click online, verify the size and specifics of your order, click once more and you are done. It is simple, easy, fast, and effective. Many times investors will take this simplicity for granted and will rush through the trade entry process thinking, "I have done this 100 times before and it is the same every time." But when you rush, that's when accidents happen. When you are entering any trade, there are four major factors that you need to check and double-check before placing a trade: The correct symbol (especially important in options trading), the correct action, the correct or desired size of the trade, and the proper order type.

The Correct Symbol

This is usually a very easy error to catch and a very simple one to correct. When you are entering an order to buy a stock, your broker's tools might automatically pull up some side information on the position. You will notice right away if the price is off or if you mistyped one letter. Verifying the symbol is much more important when entering an options trade, whether you are purchasing a protective put or selling the near term call option to generate income.

In Chapter 1, we reviewed the notation for the options symbols. If one letter is entered incorrectly you could be purchasing a two month out put instead of a six month out put as you had planned, or you could be placing an order to sell an in-the-money call when you were attempting to sell the out-of-the-money call. Over the years we have heard dozens of stories from investors who changed the whole dynamic of a position with one errant keystroke. Again, this is an easy error to catch but you always want to double-check the symbols before you click the last "Place Trade" button.

The Correct Action

When entering a protective strategy as outlined in this text, you are either buying to open shares of stock, buying to open put contracts, and potentially selling to open call contracts. Entering the wrong action can completely reverse the sentiment of the trade. If you accidentally enter the order as sell to open shares of stock, you are entering into a bearish trade. If you place a sell to open order for the put option, you are placing a naked put trade and the monetary option requirement would increase drastically. If you accidentally select buy to open for the call, you will purchase a near term call which will put you into a double bullish strategy. This may seem like extremely basic material to review, but the basics are the most important part of any trade. You always want to verify that you have selected the correct action when buying or selling any security.

The Correct Size

The online tools at your broker will most likely catch this mistake before you do. If you were placing an order to purchase 500 shares of stock but entered an extra zero, making the order 5,000 shares, you might see a message from your broker letting you know that you are exceeding your available funds. If you had the available funds for the larger trade, you would likely still notice the larger total cost when you were verifying the order.

When placing the protective put trade, there are some simple mistakes that can be made. Entering the wrong number of protective contracts can help you or it can hurt you. If you entered the order for more contracts than the amount of shares you own, you simply purchased extra protection. If the stock falls in price, this would benefit your trade, as you have the protection in place and at the same time, the extra puts are gaining in value. If you entered the order for less contracts than the amount of shares you own, the position won't be fully protected. If the stock drops, you could have a larger loss than you initially anticipated.

When selling to open the call option for the collar spread trade, it is important to sell the number of contracts equivalent to the number of shares in your account. Selling a lower number of contracts will not cause you any problems aside from lowering the total amount of income you are generating against the married put position. If you accidentally place an order to sell more contracts than are covered by the shares of stock, part of your short call position will be naked and you could suffer a significant loss. If you are trading these positions in a retirement account, your broker's tools will inform you that you are unable to place the trade. You probably will not be approved to trade naked calls in your retirement account and the computer will recognize that. If you are trading in a cash account that allows naked call trading, you still want to avoid using this strategy as a ratio trade where you have more short calls than shares to cover those calls. Trading naked calls is a bearish strategy. The stocks you are screened for in these techniques are slightly bullish. Selling extra calls that are uncovered might cause the position to suffer a large loss even if the stock moves in the desired direction.

Proper Order

When you place an order, you will have the choice to place a "Market Order" or a "Limit Order." Placing a market order means you are willing to pay the listed ask price when you are buying the stock or the put option, and that you will most likely receive the listed bid price when selling the call. If the market order was filled at price levels where you still had the maximum risk and return percentage that matched your criteria, then it is not a concern. But if the prices adjusted slightly from when you found the trade using the SmartSearchXL tool to when you placed the trade with your broker, your maximum risk might be slightly higher and the return might be slightly lower.

It is a better practice to use a "Limit Order" when buying the stock, buying the put, or selling the call. This will allow you to slightly lower your total cost basis and potentially generate a higher premium. We strongly advise that you use a limit order when purchasing the far out put option. Options that are further out in time will tend to have a wider bid/ask spread, due in part to lower option volume and open interest. You may be able to reduce the cost of the put by placing a limit order at a price that is between the listed bid and the listed ask price. This would lower the maximum risk for the position, but if the order does not get filled right away, you may be holding shares of stock without the protection in place. If your limit order is not filled within the first few minutes, you might consider cancelling and replacing the limit order at a different price. Some brokers may even allow you to enter the different legs of the position together as a married put or a collar spread. If this is the case, you might be able to enter the limit order as a net debit, the combined total of the price of the stock, the cost of the put, and the premium received from selling the call.

If you select a limit order, you will then be able to select the duration. The two most common durations are *day order* or *good 'till canceled*. The day order will stay in place until the order is filled at your limit price or the market closes. The good 'till canceled order will typically remain an open order with your broker until the position is filled or you select to cancel the order. Some other duration orders are *immediate or cancel* (the order will be canceled if it is not immediately filled) and *fill or kill* (which is similar to the previous order). You can also select the *all or none* requirement when placing the trade. This tells your broker that you want to be filled for the entire order as entered and you do not want to be partially filled.

Once you checked and double-checked the specifics of your order, click "Place Order" or "Trade." If your order is not filled in a reasonable time frame, simply cancel and replace the trade at a different limit price.

BENEFITS OF TECHNOLOGY

This may seem like a lot to double-check when placing an order for a married put trade or a collar spread trade. It is much safer to err on the side of caution rather than place an incorrect order that will change the dynamic of the trade or the risk-reward profile that you were initially seeking. Your broker may have limited option tools such as a simple option chain. From that chain you might be able to simply click a link and have the option symbol transferred into an order page for you. You will still have to enter the correct number of contracts, your desired limit price, and any other restrictions you wish to place on the trade.

At PowerOptions, we have simplified this process for you. Once you have identified the married put or collar spread position that matches your specific criteria, you can link the trade directly to a potential broker using the Broker Link function from the More Information button. You can link the trade to the broker as a complete trade, or you can select to link each leg individually. After you have identified a particular trade and have used the More Information button to further research and analyze the position, click Broker Link to link your trade. For the married put trade you can leg into the position by either selecting "Buy the Stock" or "Buy the Put."

Figure 6.1 - Broker Link Selection for Married Put

Source: PowerOptions (www.poweropt.com)

For the collar spread trade you can select to enter all three legs together by selecting "Collar" or you can choose to enter the first part of the position as a "covered call." You can also choose to leg into each separately by selecting "Buy Stock," "Sell Call," or "Buy Put."

When you select one of these trade actions, you will be linked to a secure login page for your personal trading account. Once you log on, the trade entry page will be pulled up with the stock symbol and option symbols already filled in for you. The correct action for each leg of the trade has also been selected in the trade entry page. You now just have to set and check the quantity for the shares of stock and the option contracts and adjust the prices if you wish to place a limit order.

Figure 6.2 – Broker Link Selection for Collar Spread

More Info	Company Name	Stock Sym	Last Stock Price & Chg	Call Symbol	Ca S Days
▶	Wal-Mart Stores Inc.	WMT	57.92 (+0.24)	WMTHA	08 AUC
▶	S	**Wal-Mart Stores Inc.**	(+0.04)	SAPHL	08 AUC

BrokerLink	▶	Collar
Stock Chart	▶	Covered Call
Company Info	▶	Buy the Stock
Option Chain		Sell the Call
Search by Symbol		
Research	▶	Buy the Put
Calculators	▶	Account Overview

Source: PowerOptions (www.poweropt.com)

Once you have entered in your trade specifics and limit requirements, click the "Preview Order" button. This will link you to the trade preview page so you can double-check the symbols, shares, contract size and limit prices that match your requirements.

If you notice an error, simply click "Change Order" and you will be transferred back to the previous entry page. Once you are confident that the order size and limits match your desired trade, click "Place Orders." The order will be electronically placed with your broker. You can check the orders page to see if your order has been filled. You can also use the Broker Link function to place trades from the PowerOptions Option Chain tool, the Search By Symbol tool, and the Strategy Search Summary tool.

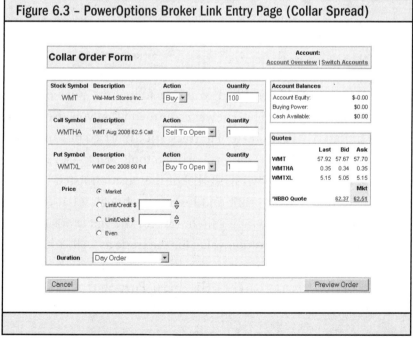

Figure 6.3 – PowerOptions Broker Link Entry Page (Collar Spread)

Source: PowerOptions (www.poweropt.com)

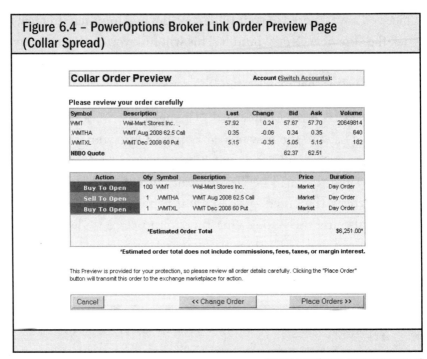

Figure 6.4 – PowerOptions Broker Link Order Preview Page (Collar Spread)

Collar Order Preview   Account (Switch Accounts):

Please review your order carefully

Symbol	Description	Last	Change	Bid	Ask	Volume
WMT	Wal-Mart Stores Inc.	57.92	0.24	57.67	57.70	20649814
.WMTHA	WMT Aug 2008 62.5 Call	0.35	-0.06	0.34	0.35	640
.WMTXL	WMT Dec 2008 60 Put	5.15	-0.35	5.05	5.15	182
NBBO Quote				62.37	62.51	

Action	Qty	Symbol	Description	Price	Duration
Buy To Open	100	WMT	Wal-Mart Stores Inc.	Market	Day Order
Sell To Open	1	.WMTHA	WMT Aug 2008 62.5 Call	Market	Day Order
Buy To Open	1	.WMTXL	WMT Dec 2008 60 Put	Market	Day Order

Estimated Order Total $6,251.00

*Estimated order total does not include commissions, fees, taxes, or margin interest.

This Preview is provided for your protection, so please review all order details carefully. Clicking the "Place Order" button will transmit this order to the exchange marketplace for action.

| Cancel | << Change Order | Place Orders >> |

Source: PowerOptions (www.poweropt.com)

Once the order has been filled, you can follow the position using your broker's portfolio view, but we recommend that you also use the PowerOptions My Portfolio tool to track your married put and collar spread trades. The PowerOptions Portfolio tools will track each position as a linked position with all legs of the position listed together. You can see the overall profit and loss on each leg and at the same time view the total liquidation gain or loss for the whole position and the potential future expiration value for the trade as well. You can set upper and lower stop limits on a variety of values for both the stock and the option positions. The "Historical Portfolio" will track the unrealized gains of your open positions while also showing a record of your closed positions. This is a very useful feature when tax season is approaching.

REVIEW

Now that you are ready to start using married puts and collar spread strategies, you first need to apply with your broker, who should be able to tell you about the requirements for each level and help you to determine which level you qualify for. Generally, you will be able to use these protective strategies at Level I and Level II.

With internet trading technology, you will likely place a lot of trades online. While this makes things very easy, it is important to check and double-check that all the details of your trade are correct, including the symbol, action, size, and proper order. Luckily, PowerOptions simplifies things for you. After using PowerOptions to choose your trade, you can immediately place the trade with a broker and then use the "My Portfolio" feature to track your trade—all through PowerOptions. In addition, from the PowerOptions "My Portfolio" tool, you can link directly to the "Position Analysis" tool for your entered positions. This tool will break down the current gain or loss on the position based on your initial costs for the trade, but most important, it will show you the potential roll out opportunities for your position based on the suggested management techniques that we will now discuss.

Chapter 7

MANAGEMENT TECHNIQUES AND MONITORING THE TRADE

These protective strategies are fantastic methods for preserving capital and limiting potential losses. In order to maximize profit in these positions, you may need to actively adjust the position, depending on the type of protective strategy you entered and your desire to hold the stock for an extended period of time. Some of the longer term married put and collar spreads may not reach a profit level for an extended period of time. In this chapter we want to go over some of the adjustments you can use on the various combinations to maximize profit or eliminate risk on the position, as well as identify some very useful tools to help you manage each position.

MANAGING THE STANDARD MARRIED PUT POSITION

As discussed in the earlier chapters, the near term, standard married put trade is essentially a hit or miss trade. You have purchased shares of stock and purchase an out-of-the-money, near term 30 day out put option. Your maximum risk might be in the range of 10 percent to

20 percent, depending on how far out-of-the-money you purchased the put and the price of the option. If you purchased a more volatile stock, even the deep out-of-the-money put option would have an inflated ask price.

In the simplest terms, all married put positions have three potential outcomes at expiration.

1. The stock will be trading below the put strike price at expiration. Without any management techniques, you would realize the maximum loss for the position.

2. The stock will be trading above the put strike price but below the break even point. You will realize a small loss on the trade and you can continue holding the stock or simply liquidate the position.

3. The stock will be trading above the break even point and you will realize a profit on the position. You can liquidate the position and take the profit or continue to hold the stock if you are still bullish on the company.

The example near term, standard married put trade showed purchasing shares of XYZ at $50.00 per share while at the same time purchasing a 1-month out, 45 strike put for $0.50 per contract. The break even point for this example trade was $50.50. Although this is fairly low, you only have 30 days for the stock to move above the break even before the protection expires. If the stock falls below the put strike price (a 10 percent drop in 30 days), you may consider simply exiting the position. You entered the position thinking the stock would move up in price, but something must have happened to cause the quick decline. This might not be the bullish stock you should be trading.

Possible Management for Near Term, Standard Married Put

Scenario 1: The stock falls below $45.00 per share at expiration or during the expiration period. At expiration, you may simply want to exercise the put and sell your shares at $45.00. You would realize the maximum loss on the position, but you would not incur any further losses if you decided to hold the stock and it continued to fall. If you are still bullish on the stock, you could sell the put for any intrinsic value, then purchase a lower strike put further out in time. Remember, purchasing the protection month by month will greatly increase your annualized cost of protection. If the stock continues to fall, you will still be taking losses on a monthly basis.

Scenario 2: The stock is trading between $45.00 and $50.50 (break even) at expiration. In this scenario, you would not realize the maximum loss, but you would still have a loss on the position. The put option would expire worthless and you could sell to close the stock for a small loss. You could also let the put expire, hold the stock, and then purchase another out-of-the-money put option for the next expiration month. Again, this will continue to increase your annualized cost of protection and would raise the break even price for the position. You could attempt to lower the break even by selling a call against the stock, thus entering into a collar spread trade.

Scenario 3: The stock rises above $50.50 at expiration. If you are comfortable with the return, simply sell to close the stock and let the put expire worthless. You can then reuse that capital to reinvest into a new position for the next expiration. You could also hold on to the stock if you think it will continue to move up in price and purchase another put option, potentially at a higher strike to maximize the protection. You know by now that this will simply increase your annualized cost of protection while increasing the break even point.

These management techniques may seem overly simple, but that is the problem with using near term protective puts. Some strategists will teach you to use elaborate strategies to repair a near term position, such as using ratio spreads or various other combinations, but this only increases the complexity of the trade. You may have to put up more capital to cover one of these combinations and increase the total risk of the trade, even with the protection still in place. This defeats the purpose of a protective strategy.

MANAGING THE STANDARD COLLAR SPREAD

The same management techniques and limitations apply to the standard collar spread. If the stock fell below $45.00 per share at expiration, you could apply the same concepts from Scenario 1 in the standard married put management. The only difference is that you could also choose to sell another at-the-money or out-of-the-money call against the stock after the lower strike put has been purchased.

If the stock stagnates and remains below the break even point but above the put strike price, you could simply buy a new put for the next month's expiration and sell another at-the-money or out-of-the-money call. Again, this would continue to increase your annualized cost of insurance, but you should still be able to collect a call premium that will pay for the monthly insurance fee.

If the stock price rises above the call strike price, you can either let the position be assigned for the maximum profit or buy to close the call. This will cancel the obligation to deliver shares of stock, but the put option will also expire. You can now decide to roll up the

standard collar spread by purchasing a higher strike put
month out and selling another at-the-money or out-of
call option. If the stock continues to rise, you can continue this pattern, but you would be limiting the maximum potential while at the same time maximizing the annual cost of insurance. This is not a fundamentally sound practice for investors.

MANAGING THE RECOMMENDED MARRIED PUT TRADE

Say that you have just entered a far out, in-the-money married put position. You have limited your maximum risk and have possibly 6 to 12 months before expiration. This gives the stock plenty of time to move up above the break even point so you can realize a profit. With six months or more of limited risk in place, you could pack your bags and take a vacation. This would be a great strategy to limit your gains and realize the limited maximum loss on the married put position.

Let's refer back to the suggested 6 month out, in-the-money married put trade.

Buy 100 shares of XYZ at $50.00 per share
Buy 1 contract, 6 month out 55 strike put for $7.75
Cost per share = $57.75
Total Cost = $5,775
Maximum Risk per share = $2.75
Maximum Risk = $275
Percent Maximum Risk = 4.8 percent
Break Even Point = $57.75
Percent to Break Even = 15.5 percent

We mentioned earlier that the average yearly growth of the market is 10 percent per year. Annualized averages are smoothed and there will be short periods of time during the year where a stock might gain 20 percent, then in the next few months lose 30 percent. It is important to reiterate this average because you should not expect too large of a gain in the stock price over a 6 month period. It is an unrealistic expectation to think the stock would gain 15.5 percent in 6 months. And that gain would simply mean you broke even on the trade. You would not have realized any profit.

For argument's sake, let's assume that the stock price rose 8 percent in the first month. Stock XYZ is now trading at $54.00 per share and you still have 5 months of protection in place. Since the stock has gained in price, the put option has naturally declined in value. You can simply assume that the stock will continue to rise and that the put option will end up expiring worthless. Even if the stock falls, you are still not at risk for more than 4.8 percent of the initial capital that was invested.

Before we simply call it a day on those assumptions, let's take a look at the total value of the married put position after the stock rose 8 percent after the first month.

Stock XYZ at $54.00 per share

Gain on Stock = $4.00 (8 percent)
Estimated 55 Strike Put Value (5 months remaining) = $5.20
Loss on Put Option = $2.55
Total Liquidation Value = Current Stock Price + Current Put Price = $59.20
Total Liquidation Profit / Loss = Liquidation Value – Initial Cost = $1.45 Profit

How did we make money on this position? Shouldn't the put option have dropped in price as much as the stock rose in price? The stock gained $4.00 in value, so shouldn't the put option have lost $4.00 in intrinsic value? If you had entered a near term, in-the-money put trade, the protective put would have lost $4.00 of intrinsic value and all time value would have decayed. This is the advantage of purchasing in-the-money put options that are far out in time for protection.

You initially purchased the 6 month out, 55 strike put for $7.75. At the time, the stock was trading at $50.00 per share. The put ask price consisted of $5.00 of intrinsic value and $2.75 of time value. Now that the stock is trading at $54.00 per share after one month, the 55 strike put option has only $1.00 of intrinsic value and $4.20 of time value.

But how can time value increase as time passes? The answer to that question was explained in Chapter 1. Options that are at-the-money, or closest to the stock price, will have the highest percentage time value. Refer back to Table 3.3, the percentage time value comparison for near month puts. This table showed that the 1 strike out-of-the-money put option had a time value of 1 percent, the 1 strike in-the-money put option had a time value of 2 percent and the at-the-money put option had a time value of 4.5 percent. In this example, the in-the-money put option was purchased for $7.75. The time value was $2.75, or 5.5 percent of the underlying stock price. As the stock moved up in price, the 55 strike put became less in-the-money and was close to at-the-money. The same wide discrepancy that was shown in Table 3.3 applies to the far out options as well. The 55 strike put option lost $4.00 of intrinsic value but gained $1.45 in time value because the put option is now at-the-money. Notice that the gain in time value is the same as the liquidation profit you now have on the example trade.

The trade might as well be liquidated now that a profit of $1.45 could be realized. This would yield a 2.5 percent return after a 30-day time period. Why would you want to do that? You still have 5 months of protection in place limiting the maximum loss on the trade. Now that the stock has moved up in price, you should look to generate income to lower the cost of the insurance. These management methods of the recommended married put trade are based on some of the techniques used by Kurt Frankenberg at RadioActive Trading. For deeper insight into potential income generating techniques, visit www.radioactivetrading.com.

STOCK INCREASES IN PRICE – FIRST CONSIDER SELLING A CALL OPTION

The most popular options investment strategy to generate income on a long stock position is to sell a call option against those shares. When a call is sold against shares of stock, it is called a *covered call trade* (refer back to Figure 2.2). Selling the call option obligates you to deliver shares of stock at the call strike price. You will receive a premium, or income, in return for providing that obligation. With the stock now trading at $54.00 per share, you could look to sell either the at-the-money or out-of-the-money near term call options.

1 month out 55 strike call option expected price = $1.50
1 month out 60 strike call option expected price = $0.30

Since we only have 100 shares, we would only sell 1 contract of either option. Depending on your commission costs, the 1 month out 60 strike call might not generate as much income as you would like. If you sell 1 contract, you would only receive $30.00 in income. Even if your commission costs were as low as $5.00 per contract, this is still a negligible amount of income. If the stock continues to rise and your shares of stock are assigned at $60.00, you would have a profit of $2.25 over the initial cost basis of $57.75. Plus, you keep the $0.30 per share in income ($30.00) that was generated from selling the call option. If the shares were assigned, you could still sell to close the put option and increase the profit even more.

If you sold the 1 month out 55 strike call, you could generate $150.00 in income. This pays for more than half of the $275.00 in time value you initially paid for the insurance of the put option. There is a risk with selling a call option that is equal to the strike price of the protective put option. If you were assigned at expiration, you would deliver your shares of stock at $55.00 per share. You would keep the $1.50 premium you received for selling the call. The value of assignment would be $56.50 per share. Your initial cost basis for the married put trade was $57.75, however. You would be assigned for a realized loss of -$1.15…or would you? Remember, you still have a long put option with 4 months left to expiration (The initial put was purchased 6 months out in time. In the first month, the stock rose 8 percent. You then sold a 1 month out call option. We are now at the call option expiration, so our put still has 4 months remaining to expiration). If the stock was trading just above $55.00, the remaining value of the put option could more than cover the -$1.15 loss. However, if the stock gapped up to $70.00 and you were assigned at $55.00, the put option would now be deep out-of-the-money and would have little value remaining.

Instead of selling the near term call option, you could consider selling the 2 month out call option against the married put position.

2 month out 55 strike call option expected price = $2.60
2 month out 60 strike call option expected price = $1.10

If the 2 month out 60 strike call option were sold, you would generate $110.00 of income. This is just shy of half of the initial time value you paid for the protective put option. If you were assigned at $60.00 in the next 60 days, you would have a profit of $2.25 per share and you would still keep the $1.10 per share income you received for selling the call option.

If you sold the 2 month out 55 strike call option, you would receive $2.60 per share, which almost covers the cost of the insurance. If you were assigned, you would receive $55.00 per share and keep the $2.60 premium. The value of assignment would be $57.60 per share, which is -$0.15 less than the initial cost basis. However, you still have a long put option with 3 months left to expiration. If the stock is trading just above $55.00 per share, the remaining put value should more than cover the -$0.15 loss on the position.

This management technique allows you to generate income to lower the overall cost basis of the position. The premium you receive is helping to pay for the cost of insurance. If the stock continues to rise above the sold call strike price, you should consider rolling the call option. This would consist of buying to close the sold call and selling to open a new call further out in time at the same or higher strike price (For tips on rolling the call option, visit our Tip Sheet on rolling covered call positions at http://www.poweropt.com/tipsheet4a.asp).

The general rules of thumb for selling a call option to generate income on a married put position are:

1. Wait for the stock to rise 5 to 8 percent before selling the call option.

2. Only sell calls that are 1 to 2 months out in time (going too far out will lower the annualized return that can be generated).

3. Look for calls where you will receive at least one-third the cost of insurance.

4. If the stock continues to rise above the sold call strike price, consider rolling up the call option to generate more income and take advantage of the stock appreciation.

STOCK INCREASES IN PRICE – ALSO CONSIDER ADJUSTING THE PUT OPTION

In the last section we explained how the in-the-money put option would gain in time value as the stock rises in price. As the purchased put option becomes more at-the-money, you will lose intrinsic value, but the time value increase can offset that loss. With a 5 percent or 8 percent increase in the stock, you could consider selling to close the put option and buying to open a 60 strike put option in the same expiration month as the initial put. Because of the shift in time value, you can sometimes gain income from this transaction.

Sell to Close 5 month out 55 strike put for $5.20
Buy to Open 5 month out 60 strike put for $7.73
New Cost of Insurance = $2.53
New Adjusted Cost Basis = $60.28
Total At Risk = $0.28 (0.4 percent of cost basis)

The 55 strike put option is at-the-money, meaning it has a very high percentage time value. The 60 strike put option is in-the-money, therefore, the percentage time value is very low. By selling to close the 55 strike put option and buying to open the 60 strike put option, you have gained time value. You could also say that you have earned time value profit. This management technique allows you to limit the percent maximum risk while having 5 months of protection still in place.

STOCK INCREASES IN PRICE – MOVE THE PUT CLOSER IN

Another technique that can be applied is to move the put closer in time. You can sell to close the 5 month out put option and buy to open a near term, 55 strike call option. This will allow you to take advantage of the increased time value of the initial purchased put option and once again generate income.

Sell to Close 5 month out 55 strike put for $5.20
Buy to Open 1 month out 55 strike put for $2.80
Total Premium Earned = $2.40
New Effective Cost Basis = $55.35

The $2.40 in premium earned from this adjustment lowers the cost basis of the position to $55.35. If the stock begins to fall, the most you have at risk is $0.35, or 0.6 percent of the adjusted cost basis. However, you have limited the time of protection to only 30 days. This might be a good time to sell the 1 month out 55 strike call option. You would receive a premium of $1.50, thus covering the total at risk value. By moving the put in time and selling the same strike call option, you have entered a conversion spread (further discussed in Chapter 8). If you are assigned at expiration, you will deliver the shares of stock at $55.00 per share but you will also keep the $1.15 profit.

$1.50 premium received - $0.35 new at-risk value = $1.15 total profit

If the stock falls in price, you can exercise the put option and sell the shares of stock at $55.00. Again, you keep the $1.15 profit and collect $55.00 per share. If the stock moves up or down you are guaranteed a profit of $1.15.

Looking at the expected call prices, it might seem that selling the 2 month out 55 strike call option would result in a higher guaranteed profit. You could sell the 2 month out 55 strike call for $2.60, guaranteeing a profit of $2.25 if you were assigned at expiration since the new cost basis is only $55.35. The problem with that logic is that the new purchased put only has 30 days to expiration. If you sold the 2 month out call option you would not have any insurance for the last 30 days. When managing the married put position, you never want to sell a call option that has an expiration date further out than the expiration date of the put option.

The management technique of moving the put closer in time should only be used if you are expecting to exit the position in that expiration month. If you decide to hold on to the position and purchase a new put further out in time, you would increase the cost of insurance. You would still be able to manage the position over time, but your cost basis would be much higher.

STOCK DROPS IN PRICE – LOWER THE PUT STRIKE PRICE

If the stock falls in price, the put option will gain in intrinsic value. If the put option becomes too deep in-the-money, it will trade at a parity, or 1:1 relationship with the stock price. If stock XYZ dropped to $25.00 in value, the put option may be worth $30.10. This is a significant gain in the put option, but there was just as significant a decrease in the underlying stock. If the position were liquidated, you would receive $30.10 for selling the put option and $25.00 for selling the shares of stock. The liquidation value would be $55.10, resulting in a loss of $2.65 from the initial cost basis. This is an extreme situation, however, and you would have managed the position before that large of a decline in the stock price.

Typically, the married put position should be managed when the stock drops 5 to 8 percent in price. Let's use our initial example, but assume the stock price had fallen 8 percent in the first month.

After 1 month (roughly 30 days)
Stock XYZ trading at $46.00 per share
Estimated 55 strike put value (5 months remaining) = $10.06
Total Liquidation Value = $56.06
Total Liquidation Profit and Loss = -$1.69

As you still have 5 months of protection remaining, you would not want to liquidate the position and realize a loss. You can sell the put option to take advantage of the increased intrinsic value, then buy to open a lower strike put option for protection.

Sell to Close 5 month out 55 strike put at $10.06
Buy to Open 5 month out 50 strike put at $6.34
Total Premium Earned = $3.72
New Effective Cost Basis = $54.03
Total At Risk = $4.03 (7.5 percent of cost basis)

This increased the total value at risk, but you were able to earn $3.72 in premium from selling the gain of intrinsic value. The adjusted position still has a limited maximum risk and 5 months remaining to expiration. One of the advantages of this management method is if the stock rebounds. With the lower strike put option in place you can participate more fully in the recovery of the stock.

If the stock continues to move down, you can continue to lower the strike price of the put option, earning premium from the increased intrinsic value. You may also consider selling a bearish options spread against the married put to generate income as the stock falls in price. Although you can keep adjusting the position, you want to have an exit strategy in place. When you entered the trade, you expected the stock to move up in price. The purchased put option provides excellent insurance, but you need the stock to rise to realize the full profit potential of the trade. Eventually, you may just want to cut your losses, liquidate the position, and look for other opportunities that could yield a better profit.

LONG-TERM PROTECTIVE STRATEGIES
Managing the 12 Month or Further Out in Time Married Put

The same techniques discussed above apply to the married put positions where the put option is further out in time. The obvious advantage of purchasing put options that are 12 months or more out in time is that you have given yourself more time to manage the position as outlined above. A second advantage of using protective put options that are a year or more out in time is that the far out options tend to retain more of their value as time passes. The further out in time the put option, the less it will be affected by daily fluctuations in the stock price. Another advantage of using far out put options and managing them is that the daily cost of insurance will be much lower. Even when you roll the strike price of the put option up or down, you will still have a lower daily cost.

Following these management techniques in either situation will give you the opportunity to lower the cost basis of the initial position, generate income, and in some cases, put you in a position to participate more fully if the stock increases or recovers from a previous decline.

Managing the Recommended Long Term Debit Collar Trade

Would you believe us if we told you we had just covered the management techniques for the long-term debit collar? Think back to the first management technique discussed for the married put trade.

Once you sold a call against a married put position, you entered into a long-term debit collar spread. A far out, in-the-money put option has been purchased and an out-of-the-money near term call option has been sold. This is the structure for the long-term debit collar.

As the stock rises in price, you can adjust the call option just as you would manage a covered call. You can buy to close the initial call and then sell to open a higher strike call further out in time. At the same time, you can maneuver the put as outlined above to earn time value premium. As the stock gains in price, you can sell to close the initial put and buy to open a higher strike put. As previously shown, the initial put option is now at-the-money and has increased time value. The higher strike, in-the-money put option will have a lower time value. You will still have limited protection and you are generating income from the sale of the new call option and from rolling the put option.

If the stock price falls, you can buy to close the call option for a lower premium and adjust the put to a lower strike price. Purchasing back the call option at a lower cost allows you to keep a large percentage of the initial premium received. Rolling down the put option will also generate some premium and help lower the initial cost basis.

Trading Tip: Beware of the Emotional Factor

Do not get reckless and sell a call option that has a lower strike than the put option you purchased! If you need further help on rules of thumb for rolling a covered call position and how that applies to the collar spread, you can access the Tip Sheet for following up a covered call position at http://www.poweropt.com/tipsheet4a.asp.

If you are following the stock down in price, you may be tempted to sell a lower strike at-the-money call to collect the higher premium. This may seem like a good idea, but if the stock rebounds you may get assigned and be locked into a loss. Only sell the call option that is equal to or greater than the strike price of the protected put option.

TECHNOLOGY MAKES IT SIMPLE

Once you have placed a married put or collar spread trade, the positions can be tracked in your brokerage account. In addition to those positions, you might have several other long stock holdings or other options investments. Many brokerage houses will lump all options transactions together and all of the stock transactions together in a portfolio view. This makes it very difficult to see the total married put or collar spread liquidation value. We recommend that you track

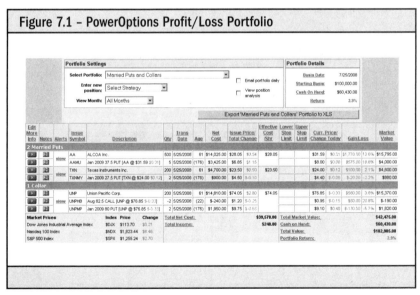

Figure 7.1 – PowerOptions Profit/Loss Portfolio

Source: PowerOptions (www.poweropt.com)

these positions using the PowerOptions Portfolio tool to help you track and manage these positions.

The PowerOptions portfolio tool will show the married put and collar spread trades as linked positions. You will be able to view all legs of the position together in one simple view.

As you can see, the PowerOptions portfolio tool displays two linked married put transactions and one collar spread transaction. The initial cost basis for all legs are shown, as is the current price and the gain and loss for each leg. The total gain and loss for the portfolio is also shown in the upper right hand corner and in the lower right hand corner. Right now there is an unrealized 2.9 percent gain for the

---

Figure 7.2 – Liquidation and Expiration Profit and Loss

Pos. Cost	Liq. Value	Liquidation Gain/Loss		Exp. Value	Expiration Gain/Loss	
$17,450.00	$19,870.00	$2,420.00	13.9%	$18,750.00	$1,300.00	7.4%
$5,600.00	$5,674.00	$74.00	1.3%	$5,500.00	$-100.00	-1.8%
$16,520.00	$16,998.00	$478.00	2.9%	$17,089.34	$569.34	3.4%

Liquidation Value:	$42,542.00	Expiration Value:	$41,339.34
Cash on Hand:	$60,430.00	Cash on Hand:	$60,430.00
Total Value:	$102,972.00	Total Value:	$101,769.34
Portfolio Return:	3.0%	Portfolio Return:	1.8%

Source: PowerOptions (www.poweropt.com)

entire portfolio. Notice in the upper part of Figure 7.1, near the center of the page, the two empty check boxes. The second box is "View Position Analysis." When this box is checked, some additional columns will be added to the portfolio view. The new columns calculate the current liquidation loss and potential future expiration value of the entire position rather than each individual leg.

For simplicity, only the liquidation values are shown. The order of the positions in Figure 7.2 is the same as in Figure 7.1. The first block is the married put liquidation and future expiration profit and loss for Alcoa position (AA). The second block is the liquidation and future expiration value for the married put trade on Texas Instruments

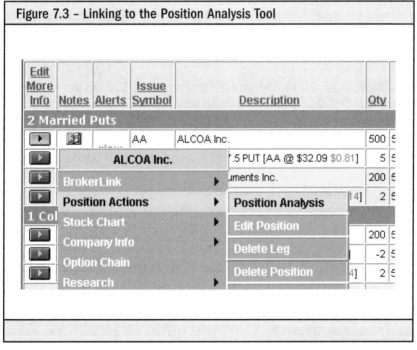

Figure 7.3 - Linking to the Position Analysis Tool

Source: PowerOptions (www.poweropt.com)

(TXN), and the third block is the values for the Union Pacific (UNP) collar spread. This is very useful for quickly comparing the current gain or loss on the entire position against the potential future expiration value.

Arguably one of the most powerful features of the PowerOptions Portfolio tool is the Position Analysis tool. The Position Analysis tool will calculate for you all potential roll out opportunities that were discussed. Simply click on the More Information button to the left of the position, select Position Actions and Position Analysis. We will look at the Alcoa (AA) married put position in this example.

The Position Analysis tool will show the initial entry values for the position and the equations used for the Original Position Cost, Current Liquidation Value, and Future Expiration Value. Beneath the position recap and profit and loss equations are the potential roll out opportunities. The original Alcoa (AA) position was:

On May 25, 2008 bought 500 shares AA at $28.05 per share
On May 25, 2008 bought 5 contracts January 2009 37.5 put for
$11.20
Total Cost Basis = $39.25
Total At Risk = $1.75 (4.5 percent of cost basis)

Alcoa's stock price has moved up to $32.02 per share, or 14.4 percent from the initial price. Linking to the Position Analysis tool allows us to view the possible roll out opportunities for this position.

As you can see in Figure 7.4, the management techniques for the increase in the stock price are shown. The first roll out opportunity is for the available calls that could be sold against the position. The near term August and September 37.5 strike calls are shown as well as the September 40 strike call. The roll out field calculates for you the

Figure 7.4 - Married Put Roll Out Opportunities on PowerOptions

Roll Out Opportunities...

Your stock has risen by 14.2%, you may want to consider writing a covered call for income. You could sell to open one of the below calls...

More Info	Call Symbol	Expire/Strike & Days To Exp.	Call Bid	w/o Put % Assnd	% Assnd	% Assnd Annual	% Prob Above	% OTM
	AAHU	08 AUG 37.50 (22)	$0.22	-3.9%	7.8%	128.8%	$9.2%	17.1%
	AAIU	08 SEP 37.50 (57)	$0.72	-2.7%	7.8%	49.7%	$20.4%	17.1%
	AAIH	08 SEP 40.00 (57)	$0.42	3.0%	10.8%	69.1%	$12.2%	24.9%

You may want to consider rolling your existing put in. You could sell to close your existing put and buy to open one of the below puts...

More Info	Put Symbol	Expire/Strike & Days To Exp.	Put Ask	New Break Even	New Max Risk	New % Max Risk	New Max Risk /Mo
	AATH	08 AUG 40.00 (22)	$8.30	$39.85	$-0.15	-0.4%	$-0.15
	AATV	08 AUG 42.50 (22)	$10.75	$42.30	$-0.20	-0.5%	$-0.20
	AAVH	08 OCT 40.00 (85)	$8.95	$40.50	$0.50	1.2%	$0.18
	AAVV	08 OCT 42.50 (85)	$11.15	$42.70	$0.20	0.5%	$0.07
	AAUH	08 SEP 40.00 (57)	$8.55	$40.10	$0.10	0.2%	$0.05
	AAUV	08 SEP 42.50 (57)	$10.85	$42.40	$-0.10	-0.2%	$-0.05

You may want to consider rolling your existing put out. You could sell to close your existing put and buy to open one of the below puts...

More Info	Put Symbol	Expire/Strike & Days To Exp.	Put Ask	New Break Even	New Max Risk	New % Max Risk	New Max Risk /Mo
	YJAMH	10 JAN 40.00 (540)	$12.10	$43.65	$3.65	8.4%	$0.20

You may want to consider adding a bear call credit spread to your position. You could trade of the spreads below...

More Info	Sell Option	Expire/Strike & Days To Exp.	Buy Option	Expire/Strike & Days To Exp.	Net Credit	Adj. Cost Basis	New Max Risk	New % Max Risk	New Max Risk /Mo
	AAHZ	08 AUG 32.5 (22)	AAHG	08 AUG 35.0 (22)	$0.69	$38.56	$1.06	2.7%	$1.06

Source: PowerOptions (www.poweropt.com)

calls that match the general rules of thumb, the static and annualized return if the call is assigned, and the probability that the call will be assigned at expiration. Based on your personal risk-reward tolerance, you could choose to look for the higher premium, the higher probability, or the largest time value when selecting which call to sell.

The second section of roll out opportunities is the "Roll the Put In" management technique. Remember, you would only roll the put position to a closer expiration month if you were planning on exiting the whole position soon. You may be able to sell a call option as well once you have adjusted the put.

The third roll out shows moving the put further out in time. This gives you the advantage of having nearly the same limited maximum risk but expands the amount of time to manage the trade. Naturally, this will lower the cost of insurance per day.

The last roll opportunity shows a credit spread trade against the married put position. This will generate income today and lower the cost basis of the entire position. This roll out was only touched upon in the previous section, but there is more discussion on this technique in the next chapter.

This example shows the roll out opportunities for a stock that has moved up in price. If you are tracking a stock in the PowerOptions Portfolio tool that has dropped in price by more than 5 percent, the Position Analysis tool will show you the roll opportunities for a falling stock. You will also be able to view the various roll out opportunities for the long-term debit collar spread as well.

REVIEW

By now you can tell that the co-authors of this book strongly advocate these two protective strategies. We have seen too many investors come into the market and lose all of their available trading capital in a two or three month time span because of one major unforeseen stock decline. You should seriously consider trading these strategies as part of your investment methodology to better preserve your account capital. If you are seriously considering implementing these protective strategies, the PowerOptions tools will save you hours of research time and manual calculations. Using the patented SmartSearchXL tool, you can quickly find only those trades that match your specific investment criteria and risk threshold. You can use the Search by Symbol to quickly compare the percent maximum risk and potential return for any married put or collar combination on a given stock. You can then track the positions easily using the Portfolio tool that displays the trades as linked positions. All of the management calculations and roll out opportunities can be seen with a simple click of your mouse.

Chapter 8

SOME ADVANCED CONCEPTS

You have now been introduced to some protective strategies and seen how the risk-reward profiles of married put and collar spread trades match up against simply trading shares of stock and against some common options investing strategies. We have illustrated our recommended techniques to maximize protection while maintaining a position to effectively manage the trade, discussed the types of stocks you might want to search for, and we delved into the criteria to use in the powerful SmartSearchXL tool to find only those trades that match your personal investment ideas. We shared some tips on how to enter the trade and various management techniques to maximize profit and limit your overall risk. In this chapter, we will examine some of the alternative strategies that can be created using variations of the protective strategies discussed so far.

RATIO MARRIED PUT

Mike Phillips, the head analyst at PowerOptionsApplied (Power-Options Advisory Newsletter service — www.poweroptionsapplied.

com) noticed that the recommended married put criteria shown in Chapter 5 would identify put options with a delta in the range of -0.70. If the stock fell $1.00, the put option would only gain $0.70. In the event of a declining stock, the put option's price movement does not inversely mirror or inversely track the price of the falling stock. One to one protection is not possible if the delta of the put option is not near -1.00.

One way to modify the married put strategy to enable closer inverse tracking between the put and the stock is to purchase more put insurance. One ratio for achieving a better inverse tracking appears to be 7 to 8; that is, 700 shares of stock with 8 contracts of put protection. Since many investors cannot adequately diversify their portfolios with 700 shares of stock, a 3.5 to 4 ratio may also be used; 350 shares with 4 put contracts for insurance.

Ratio Married Put Trade
Buy 350 shares of XYZ at $50.00
Buy to Open 4 contracts, 6-month out 55 strike put at $7.75

The ratio combination of the far out, in-the-money married put strategy lowers your potential maximum risk, though the total cost may be significantly higher. As the stock falls in price, the puts will start to track the stock closer to a 1:1 delta, and the protection is increased due to the extra number of put options.

RATIO MARRIED PUT PLUS CREDIT SPREAD

Another method that can be used to limit the cost of an in-the-money, far out in time married put trade is to sell a credit spread at the same time you enter the married put trade. You can look to trade

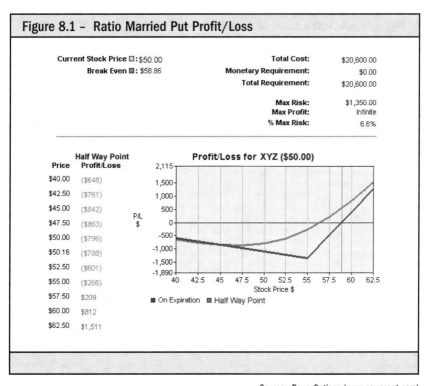

Figure 8.1 – Ratio Married Put Profit/Loss

Current Stock Price ☐: $50.00	
Break Even ■: $58.86	

Total Cost:	$20,600.00
Monetary Requirement:	$0.00
Total Requirement:	$20,600.00
Max Risk:	$1,350.00
Max Profit:	Infinite
% Max Risk:	6.6%

Profit/Loss for XYZ ($50.00)

Price	Half Way Point Profit/Loss
$40.00	($648)
$42.50	($761)
$45.00	($842)
$47.50	($863)
$50.00	($796)
$50.16	($788)
$52.50	($601)
$55.00	($266)
$57.50	$209
$60.00	$812
$62.50	$1,511

■ On Expiration ■ Half Way Point

Source: PowerOptions (www.poweropt.com)

either a bear call credit spread or a bull put credit spread depending on your sentiment of the stock. You could also try something more elaborate such as an iron condor spread or an iron butterfly spread. All four strategies will generate income against the ratio married put position, though you have to be comfortable with the adjusted risk-reward profile. To complicate things further, it might be best to only trade one contract of each option in the credit spread, condor spread, or butterfly spread.

Here is a look at adding a bear call credit spread to the ratio married put position.

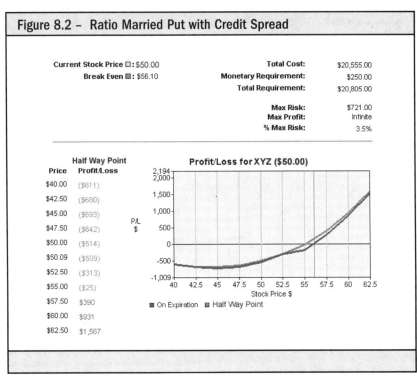

Figure 8.2 – Ratio Married Put with Credit Spread

Current Stock Price ☐: $50.00
Break Even ∎: $56.10

Total Cost:	$20,555.00
Monetary Requirement:	$250.00
Total Requirement:	$20,805.00
Max Risk:	$721.00
Max Profit:	Infinite
% Max Risk:	3.5%

Half Way Point

Price	Profit/Loss
$40.00	($611)
$42.50	($680)
$45.00	($693)
$47.50	($642)
$50.00	($514)
$50.09	($509)
$52.50	($313)
$55.00	($25)
$57.50	$390
$60.00	$931
$62.50	$1,567

Profit/Loss for XYZ ($50.00)

■ On Expiration ▨ Half Way Point

Source: PowerOptions (www.poweropt.com)

Buy 350 shares of XYZ at $50.00
Buy to Open 4 contracts, 6-month out 55 strike put at $7.75
Sell to Open 1 contract, near term 52.50 strike call at $0.75
Buy to Open 1 contract, near term 55 strike call at $0.30

By trading a credit spread, you generate $0.45 premium against the cost of the protective put options that lowers the initial cost basis, but may increase the total options requirement. When you enter a credit spread, you may have to have some cash in your account to cover the maximum risk of the spread. Many brokerage firms will not allow investors to trade credit spreads in an IRA or retirement account. However, your broker may treat the short call as being protected by 100 shares of the purchased stock. Another way to view this trade is below.

Covered Call: Long 100 shares of XYZ at $50.00
Short 1 contract $52.50 call at $0.75

Plus Other Long Options: Long 1 contract 55 call at $0.30
Long 4 contracts 55 strike, 6-month out put at $7.75 per contract
Long Stock: 250 shares of XYZ at $50.00 per share.

If you legged into the position as outlined above, you could potentially trade this in your retirement account since all four transactions should be allowed as a Level I or Level II qualification. Although adding a credit spread lowers the initial cost basis for the ratio position, you have to make sure you are comfortable with the risk-reward adjustment and that you are prepared to monitor and manage the position closely.

REVERSE COLLAR SPREAD

In Chapter 3, we told you that you could reverse the sentiment of a collar spread, turning it from a neutral to bullish position into a bearish position using a certain combination of protective puts and short calls. This is an example of just that, a collar spread with a bearish sentiment.

Reverse Collar Spread
Buy 100 shares of XYZ at $50.00
Sell to Open 1 contract, 1 month out 45 call for $5.60
Buy to Open 1 contract, 1 month out 55 put for $6.00

You have really turned the tables with this trade. Your maximum return is roughly 9 percent for a 30 day trade while you are only risking about 11 percent of the total capital you invested on the trade.

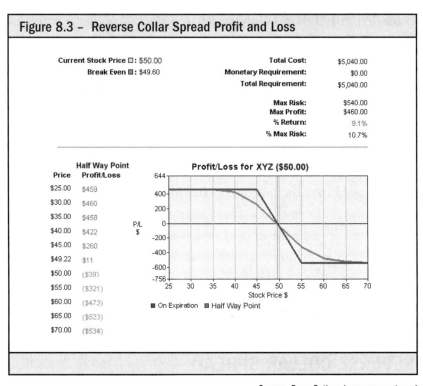

Figure 8.3 – Reverse Collar Spread Profit and Loss

Current Stock Price ☐: $50.00		Total Cost:	$5,040.00
Break Even ■: $49.60		Monetary Requirement:	$0.00
		Total Requirement:	$5,040.00
		Max Risk:	$540.00
		Max Profit:	$460.00
		% Return:	9.1%
		% Max Risk:	10.7%

Half Way Point

Price	Profit/Loss
$25.00	$459
$30.00	$460
$35.00	$458
$40.00	$422
$45.00	$260
$49.22	$11
$50.00	($39)
$55.00	($321)
$60.00	($473)
$65.00	($523)
$70.00	($534)

Profit/Loss for XYZ ($50.00)

■ On Expiration ■ Half Way Point

Source: PowerOptions (www.poweropt.com)

You will realize the maximum return if the stock falls below $45.00 at expiration. You will realize the maximum loss if the stock goes above $55.00 at expiration. The risk-reward values are similar to the standard collar spread trade from Chapter 3, only in this trade, the risk-reward profile is reversed. You make the maximum return if the stock falls 10 percent and you hit the maximum loss if the stock rises 10 percent in the next 30 days. You have reversed the sentiment of the standard collar trade.

The reverse collar spread may be a good technique to use in a bearish market, but it is a counter intuitive strategy for an investor that is purchasing shares of stock. Think about it: over 90 percent of the capital you invested into this position is in the stock. Typically, when you buy shares of stock, you are hoping for an increase in the price to realize a profit. In this example, you have purchased $5,000 worth of stock and you are hoping that it drops 10 percent in the next 30 days so you can realize a 9 percent profit. Most investors who have a bearish sentiment on a stock will trade a short collar, which consists of shorting shares of stock, purchasing an out-of-the-money call for protection, and selling an out-of-the money put to generate income. We will not go into the specific advantages and disadvantages of the reverse collar trade in this text. Instead we will recommend that if you do have a bearish sentiment on the stock in the short term, that you use the tools on PowerOptions to compare the risk-reward of the bear call credit spread or bear put debit spread, which are parity trades to the reverse collar spread and short collar spread.

CONVERSION SPREAD

The co-authors of this book debated at some length on whether we should include this strategy in this text. A conversion spread is one of the most protective strategies that an investor can trade, but the rewards are so low that it really does not benefit a retail investor. If you have a large amount of free capital that you wish to put into one trade, a conversion spread might work for you. By large amount, we mean a *very* large amount. The conversion spread has no risk, but the potential profits are so limited that it almost does not make any sense to place the trade. This strategy is commonly used by floor traders and by some institutional holdings, but it is not a realistic trade for the retail investor.

In this collar spread technique, an investor will purchase shares of stock, sell the at-the-money call, and buy the same strike, at-the-money put for protection.

Conversion Collar Spread

Buy 100 shares of XYZ at $50.00
Sell to Open 1 contract, 1 month out 50 strike call for $2.15
Buy to Open 1 contract, 1 month out 50 strike put for $2.24

Based on our theoretical prices of the available options, a conversion spread would not work on this stock. You have agreed to sell shares of stock at $50.00, but your overall cost basis was $50.09 (the protective put cost $0.09 more than the premium you received from selling the call). If the stock drops below $50.00, you can exercise your put and sell the stock at $50.00, but you would still have a $0.09 loss. Let's assume that you entered a limit order for the call and the put and essentially reversed the costs. Your conversion spread would be:

Buy 100 shares of XYZ at $50.00
Sell to Open 1 contract, 1 month out 50 strike call for $2.24
Buy to Open 1 contract, 1 month out 50 strike put for $2.15

You have now entered into the most neutral of neutral strategies. The stock can rise in value as high as it wants and it can fall in value as low as it wants. Regardless if the stock rises to $100.00 or drops to $0.01, you are guaranteed to make $0.09 per share on the trade. If you traded only 100 shares, you are guaranteed $9.00 profit whether the stock moves up or down. But what were your commission costs? To enter the trade you had to pay a commission to buy shares of stock, pay a commission to sell the call, and another commission to purchase the put option. In order to exit the conversion, you will either be assigned at the call strike price or you will exercise the put option and sell the shares of stock. In either case, you will have to pay another stock commission. Add up your total commission costs. Are they less than $9.00? If you want to make a reasonable monetary profit trading conversion spreads, you may need to trade at least 1,000 shares and 10 contracts or more. Do you have $50,000 lying

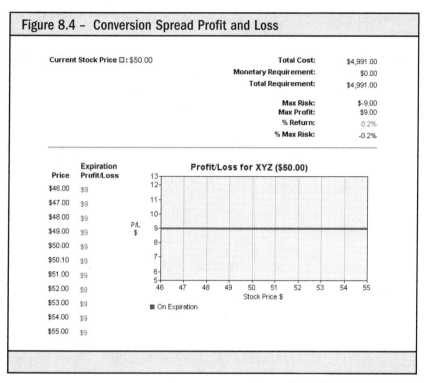

Figure 8.4 – Conversion Spread Profit and Loss

Current Stock Price ▢: $50.00		Total Cost:	$4,991.00
		Monetary Requirement:	$0.00
		Total Requirement:	$4,991.00
		Max Risk:	$-9.00
		Max Profit:	$9.00
		% Return:	0.2%
		% Max Risk:	-0.2%

Profit/Loss for XYZ ($50.00)

Price	Expiration Profit/Loss
$46.00	$9
$47.00	$9
$48.00	$9
$49.00	$9
$50.00	$9
$50.10	$9
$51.00	$9
$52.00	$9
$53.00	$9
$54.00	$9
$55.00	$9

■ On Expiration

Source: PowerOptions (www.poweropt.com)

idle in your account that you would be willing to place into one trade for a guaranteed 0.2 percent return, not including commission costs? Floor traders and institutional investors are the main users of the conversion strategy.

MARGIN COLLARS

Neither of the co-authors trade long stocks on margin. When you trade shares of stock on margin, you are borrowing shares from your broker and you will be charged a monthly interest fee on those borrowed shares. Those fees can change the dynamic of a protective married put or collar spread trade. In addition, you will not be able to use margin in a retirement or an IRA account. The advantage of trading on margin is that you are using less capital to take advantage of the stock price movement. Some brokers may allow you to borrow over 50 percent of the cost of the underlying shares. Although you only put up 50 percent of the cost, you are still covered if you wish to sell a call option to generate income. Since you used less capital to enter the position, the percentage return will be much higher. If the stock moves up and you are assigned, you only own a portion of the shares needed to fulfill the obligation. The rest will have to be borrowed from your broker, and you will have to pay interest on the amount owed.

Some brokers may only require the maximum amount at risk for the collar spread trade as collateral in a margin account. This approach is fairly new and only a few brokers have tried to adopt it. Let's take a look at our standard married put trade from Chapter 1.

Buy 100 shares of XYZ at $50.00
Buy to Open 1 contract, 1 month out 45 strike put at $0.50
Total Position Cost = $5,050
Maximum Risk = $550

In a standard margin account, you might only need $2,500 for the stock instead of $5,000 (50 percent margin account). With the new margin requirements, you might be able to enter the trade with $550, which is the total at-risk amount for the trade. Once you entered the married put with the at-risk margin, you could now sell a call option and turn the position into a margin collar. You would still receive the full premium for the call option even though you only put up a fraction of the stock price to enter the trade. Again, very few brokers use this margin technique. The individual's requirements to qualify for this type of margin might be very strict, as well. You may need to have a very large trading account, a high net worth, and lots of options trading experience. We do not recommend margin trading unless you are fully aware of the risks involved or you have some prior experience trading on margin. Contact your broker if you have any questions about margin requirements for your personal trading account.

ETF – INVERSE ETF MARRIED PUT AND COLLAR SPREADS

ETFs (Exchange Traded Funds) are investments that can be bought or sold just like shares of stock. An ETF tracks the net value of a group of similar stocks or bonds, or the ETF may track a larger broad based index. ETFs allow investors to take advantage of a strong sector or industry without having to purchase multiple stocks in that industry. Many ETFs will have an inverse or short ETF as well. The short ETF will track the inverse movement of the stock. Recently there have been many new optionable ETFs, Short (inverse) ETFs, and UltraShort ETFs (twice the inverse) released on the market. We field several questions from beginner and intermediate options investors on how to create collar spreads or protective positions using a standard ETF combined with its inverse or UltraShort ETF.

For example, many readers are probably familiar with the security SPY, the S&P Depositary Receipts Trust ETF. This ETF tracks the S&P 500 Index and the price of SPY reflects a fraction of the total net value of all stocks in that index. There are also two ETFs that are designed to track the inverse of SPY.

1. **SH**—ProShares Short S&P 500 ETF. This ETF was established to be an inverse of the S&P 500 ETF, though it is not a direct 1:1

ratio to SPY, as only about 80 percent of assets move contrary to the economics of the S&P 500 index. In general, if SPY gains $1.00, SH should drop about $0.80.

2. **SDS**—ProShares UltraShort S&P 500 ETF. The UltraShort ETFs are designed to correspond to twice the inverse of a regular ETF or index. SDS is set up to track twice the inverse of the S&P 500 index, though it too only reflects about 80 percent of assets that move contrary to the economics of the S&P 500 index.

Some may look to purchase shares of SPY while at the same time purchasing an equal number of shares of SH or SDS for protection. They will then sell calls against SPY to generate income. They are bullish on SPY and are using SH or SDS as protection in case SPY drops in price. There are some problems with this type of thinking.

- First, this is more akin to a long straddle than a protective married put or collar spread strategy.

- Second, even though SH and SDS are inverse ETFs to the S&P 500 index, they do not track SPY at exactly a 1:1 or 2:1 ratio. If SPY has a significant movement in either direction you may have a lag in the price of the inverse ETFs.

- Third, this technique requires a lot of capital. At the time this text was written, SPY was trading around $135.00 per share with SH and SDS trading around $65.00 per share. If you purchased 100 shares of the ETF and one of its inverses, you would need $20,000 available capital for one position. It might be better to purchase 100 shares of SPY and purchase a far out, in-the-money put option to protect SPY directly.

PORTFOLIO MARRIED PUT OR COLLAR SPREAD

Instead of purchasing a protective put option on each optionable stock in your portfolio, you can use put options on an index or ETF to protect your portfolio from market downdrafts. Simply look over your portfolio holdings and see if there is a common group or sector that dominates your long stock positions (the PowerOptions Portfolio Analysis tool is great for this analysis). For example, if you saw that 65 percent of your assets consisted of stocks in the S&P 500 index, you could purchase put options on that index or on SPY. If your S&P 500 stocks start to fall, the index or ETF puts will gain in value to offset those losses. If you had 5 or 6 stocks that were related to silver or gold mining operations, you could purchase put options on a mining ETF or on a metals index.

There are several problems with this type of portfolio protection. First, if you have very large positions with a large amount of capital invested, it might be very expensive to purchase a large number of put options to maximize protection. Second, the index or ETF put options will not track your positions directly. The indexes and ETF values are comprised of many different issues from a designated group. If your stock has a significant drop in price, that is only a portion of the index or ETF. You will not see as significant a change in the broader index or ETF, thus the protective puts will not offer direct protection for your stock. If there was a significant fall across the entire sector, this technique would protect the holdings in your account, but it would be much more conservative to purchase protective puts for each individual stock.

REVIEW

We wanted to show you some of the variations of the married put and collar spread strategy that you can use in your portfolio to increase protection on a single position or to have insurance in place on your entire portfolio. There are dozens of different option strategies and many variations on each strategy an investor can develop to match their personal risk-reward tolerance. Although we outlined our particular "recommended" methods for these strategies back in Chapter 3, every investor has their own individual investment goals and ideas. The co-authors strongly suggest that you employ some variation of these protective strategies in your account during these uncertain market conditions so you can better preserve your trading capital.

Chapter 9

STRATEGY REVIEW AND A MARRIED PUT TRADE IN ACTION

The purpose of this text was to introduce you to a safe and conservative methodology to trade married puts and collar spread strategies. These two protective strategies will allow you to protect 90 percent or more of the initial capital invested while you still have the ability to manage the position and generate income. These strategies are two of the safest investment methods to protect your portfolio against major losses. Over the last several years, the most common reason why people stopped trading is because they had one significant loss on a single stock. All of their profits plus a significant portion of their portfolio was wiped out because of one single stock. Some unforeseen event caused a 30, 40, or 50 percent drop in the pre-market or after-market hours. Even though they had stop losses in place they still suffered the large loss. These two strategies protect against those unforeseen events, will preserve your capital, and allow you to keep trading for a longer period of time. The chapters were placed in an order to help you understand these trades from beginning to end.

CHAPTER 1

In Chapter 1, we introduced you to options specifics and the important aspects of these two protective strategies. Buying a put option will insure shares of a long stock. The put owner has the right to sell the shares of stock at the strike price at any time between now and the expiration date. This insurance will help you greatly reduce the risk of owning shares of stock for a minimal cost. Selling a call option will allow you to generate income on a monthly basis so you can lower the cost of the position and pay for the cost of the insurance. The standard married put trade and the standard collar spread trade were introduced and compared to a long stock position. This illustrated the benefits of trading either protective strategy over simply owning shares of stock without protection in place.

CHAPTER 2

Chapter 1 answered the questions: "What are options?" and "What are married puts and collar spreads?" Chapter 2 answered the question, "Why should I use them?" Our experience has shown that most investors are averse to trading protective strategies. They just don't seem willing to pay the extra premium to add insurance to the long stock positions. However, it costs a lot more not to have insurance in place. There are many unforeseen market events that can cause a stock to drop drastically in price in just a short period of time. Without protection, an investor's available trading capital can be wiped out in one moment. Even with stop loss orders in place or in a diversified portfolio, one large loss can take months from which to recover. Other investors may feel that the more commonly used options strategies such as long calls and covered calls are less risky and more cost effective than trading married puts or collar spreads. We compared those strategies to the protective strategies as well, so you could see just how valuable these protective strategies are to any investor.

CHAPTER 3

Options give you, well, options. With all of the available expiration months and possible strike prices, how can you determine which strategy is the best for you? That all depends on your personal risk-reward threshold and how long you are willing to hold on to a position. We attempted to show you some of the more common variations of these two strategies, comparing the maximum profit, the probability of making that profit, and the maximum risk for each trade. The purpose of these protective strategies is to limit your risk and lower the daily cost of insurance while still being in a position to generate income and adjust the position. The comparisons reflected that the far out, in-the-money married put trade satisfies that purpose, as does the long-term debit collar spread strategy. These two methods allow you to significantly lower your overall risk, to offer the lowest cost of insurance per day, and to have the benefit of insurance in place for several months. This gives you an extended time period to manage the trade and adjust the position to maximize profit.

CHAPTER 4

Even though both strategies limit the total maximum risk, they are both neutral to bullish strategies. You need the stock price to rise in order to realize a profit or to be in a good position to manage the trade to reduce the cost of insurance. You can use both fundamental and technical criteria to help find these companies. Look for stocks that have a rising chart pattern and are currently in an uptrend. You also want to purchase only stocks that you would not mind owning for an extended period of time. Research the news articles and upcoming earnings releases for the company. Make sure there are no outlying circumstances that appear negative or cause you concern. At all times be cautious. You may have had success the past few months with a certain set of criteria to identify stocks, but the market is ever changing. What worked six months ago may not work in the current market (recall the OfficeMax example). Back testing a strategy can greatly help you develop your stock criteria to find positions that work in a bearish, neutral, or bullish market. You have entered a trade with limited risk, but you still need the stock price to move up in order to realize a profit.

CHAPTER 5

Once you have identified the stocks that match your criteria, you have to identify the put option that offers the desired protection, as well as potentially match the short call option that matches your requirements. You can scroll through an option chain and try this analysis by hand, but it is much easier to use the SmartSearchXL tool to identify your preferred positions in mere seconds. When screening for married puts, look for positions that are at least 5 months out in time and offer a risk of less than 9 percent. Positions with a maximum risk of less than 1 percent may be too far in-the-money. If the protective put is more than 20 percent in-the-money, it is unrealistic to expect a 15 or 20 percent gain in the next 5 or 6 months. Some stocks may have a high price increase in a short time span, but they are very speculative. With all of the criteria that you can use to identify a potential married put trade or long term debit collar spread, remember the KISS rule: Keep it Simple Simple. Start out with the basics and then adjust your criteria from there. These protective strategies can also help you lock in profits if you have a stock that has moved up in price. Although we feel these techniques are the best way to trade these strategies, nothing is guaranteed. The goal of this text is to teach you how to fish, not to hand you the fish cooked and ready to eat. There are many ways to identify a neutral to bullish stock, and every investor has their own risk-reward tolerance. But you cannot be a successful fisherman without knowing the risks of fishing blindly without a license or without the proper tools. Married puts and collar spreads give you the insurance to trade almost any stock you want, and the PowerOptions tools give you an ideal platform to identify those trades that match your individual investment ideas.

CHAPTER 6

Before you start trading these strategies, you will need to check with your broker and make sure that you are approved to trade options. Both of these strategies are allowed in most retirement accounts and IRAs. Although technology has advanced the simplicity of placing any options investment strategy, you always want to double-check your order before it placed. Make sure that you have entered the correct symbol, selected the correct action, that your position size is accurate and that you are in a reasonable range if placing a limit order. When opening a married put position, the correct action is buy the stock and buy to open the put. When entering a collar spread, the correct actions are buy the stock, buy to open the put, and sell to open the call. If your limit order does not get filled within the first hour, consider adjusting the limit order if the price still matches your risk threshold.

CHAPTER 7

Once you have entered a protected married put or collar spread strategy, you should not simply expect the stock to rise in price to earn a profit. There are many management techniques that you can use as the stock moves up or the stock moves down to earn income and help pay for the cost of the insurance. A few of these management techniques are simple but some may require calculation and comparison to options with different expiration months. The PowerOptions portfolio tools have simplified the tracking of these two protective strategies and even implemented tools to help with the roll out opportunities and management techniques. Entering one of these two protected strategies and applying the management techniques will help you preserve capital while still being able to generate a reasonable monthly income.

CHAPTER 8

We have a certain method of fishing that works for us, but there are many other ways to fish. There are various combinations, alterations, and variations of these two strategies that you can use to match your individual investing ideas. You can use ratio protection techniques, reverse the sentiment to be protected on bearish stocks, be completely neutral, or trade using margin. We do not recommend some of these techniques, but you want to find the technique that best suits your needs and annualized goals. There are many adjustments that can be made, just make sure that whatever technique you use you are still limiting your maximum risk and your positions are not too exposed.

ANOTHER REAL WORLD EXAMPLE

In September of 2007, it appeared that Hewlett Packard was doing well and continuing an upward trend. Analyst reports were positive, expecting the stock to move from the upper $40s to the $60 price range. The following married put position was established.

Transaction: September 6, 2007

Buy 1000 Hewlett Packard (HPQ) at $50.38	
Buy 10 January 09 $55 puts at	$ 8.30
Total Invested	$58.68 B/E
Insured at $55 for 499 days	- 55.00
At Risk	3.68 points or 6.27 percent

The married put setup established an insured position for HPQ. If HPQ's stock price declined to zero, the position loss would be limited to 3.68 points or 6.27 percent of the invested capital because of the January 2009 put option that we purchased for insurance. If the price of the HPQ stock had remained at $50 for the following 499 days, it could be sold at $55 with the exercise of the put option. The loss would be 3.68 points (6.27 percent), which is the cost of the put option insurance. With this position, we have 499 days to earn income from the position or observe a capital gain from a stock price increase above the put option strike price.

Generally, it is best to wait for a 5 or 10 percent move in the stock to determine the next step in the management process. At the beginning of November, HPQ's stock price was having difficulty moving above the $52 resistance level. After a month of waiting with virtually no change, a near term call option was sold.

Transaction: November 2, 2007
Price of HPQ = $52.40
Sell 10 December 07 $52.50 calls at $2.40

The call options for HPQ expired worthless on December 12, 2007. There was an opportunity to exit this position at the end of November for $0.30. In retrospect, this would have been an opportunity to exit the covered call obligation sooner, but the window of opportunity only lasted a few days. As a rule of thumb, it is a good idea to exit the sold call option position if 80 percent of the premium has been realized and there are more than a few weeks remaining until option expiration. Once the call option price went under $.50 during the month of November, the December call option should probably have been closed.

$$20\% \times 2.40 = 0.48$$

After the December expiration, a January call option was sold on the following Monday.

Transaction: December 24, 2007
Price of HPQ = $52.32
Sell 10 January 08 $52.50 calls at $1.20

The call option premium was not very attractive since there were only 27 days left before the January expiration on January 19, 2008. By January 7, the HPQ stock price declined significantly. Intel announced unfavorable industry news and the entire PC industry experienced price declines. An order was entered to exit the call option for $.05 and was executed on January 8.

Transaction: January 8, 2008
Price of HPQ = $43.19
Bought to Close 10 January 08 $52.50 calls at $.05

To summarize where we stand, the stock that we purchased at $50.38 is now worth $43.19. The stock that we expected to go to $60 is now down 7 points per share, or $7,000. This represents a 14 percent drop in the stock since purchase over 4 months ago. However, we purchased put options for the 1,000 shares purchased to provide insurance and wrote covered calls to generate income, both of which should help considerably to alleviate the decline. Below is how the numbers look so far.

Hewlett Packard stock at	$43.19 *current value*
January 2009 $55 put at	$13.00
December 2007 $52.50 CC	$ 2.40
January 2008 $52.50 CC	$ 1.15 *1.20? ✱*
Total Value January 8, 2008	$59.74

In September 2007, when this position was created, we invested $58.68, which is now worth $59.74. There was a 14 percent decline in the stock, yet the position is actually up slightly. Between the put option increasing in value and the ability to write covered calls on the stock, the position has been able to maintain its value. At this point, the position is very deeply hedged since an opposite movement in the put option cancels any movement in HPQ stock. Clearly the use of married puts and covered calls has succeeded in insuring the position against a significant loss up to this point in time. Also, the position was originally insured for a cost of 3.68 points, but by writing the December and January covered calls, we recovered 3.55 points. The insurance has been virtually paid off using these management techniques.

On January 23, HPQ's stock price declined to $40 per share during the day, and it was considered to roll down the put option to a lower strike price; but the stock rebounded over the next few days and the opportunity disappeared. The plan was to write another covered call at the $50 strike price if a market rally carried the stock over $48, but the rally stopped at about $46. HPQ's $40 stock price low was tested on February 7 with high volume but was not penetrated. The following day HPQ's stock price rebounded and formed a double bottom. At this point it appeared the $40 level would hold and it was decided to lower the put strike price for the put option.

Transaction: February 20, 2008

Price of HPQ = $44.00

Sell January 09 $55 put at $12.20
Buy January 09 $50 put at $ 8.60
$ 3.60

Rolling down the put option lowered the insurance investment cost and provided a lower break even point in case the stock continued to increase in value. The knee for the price appreciation of the stock would now yield gains after a stock price rise above $50 instead of the previous $55 level.

Near the end of February, HPQ's stock price once again crossed over $48 and created an opportunity to write another covered call. Generally a covered call is written for one month out in time in order to maximize the annualized return. However, looking at the option chain for HPQ, it was possible to receive twice the premium for the second month out in time. Therefore, there was no potential return penalty for writing the covered call for the month of April.

Transaction: February 27, 2008

Price of HPQ = $48.94

Sell April 08 $50 call at $1.60

After the April 50 call expired worthless on April 19, 2008, another covered call was sold on the first Monday after expiration for the same strike price and the next month out in time.

The HPQ stock remained flat for most of the month of April and the beginning of May, but spiked up near the middle of May. The upward spike caused some concern because the covered call strike price of $50 could force a sale of the stock once it moved in-the-money. Generally, the covered call would be bought back if the stock price moved to more than $2 or $3 in-the-money. A merger announcement between HPQ and EDS had a negative effect on HPQ's stock price and prevented it from continuing the upward trend. Subsequently, the May $50 call option expired worthless and the July $50 call option was sold. This position was 2 months out in time because the call option premium was low for the first month and twice as much for the second month out.

Transaction: May 19, 2008 with HPQ at $47
Sell July 08 $50 call at $0.80

To summarize for June 12, 2008:

Hewlett Packard stock at	$46.80
January 2009 $50 put at	$ 6.00
December 2007 $52.50 CC	$ 2.40
January 2008 $52.50 CC	$ 1.15
Income from put	$ 3.60
April 2008 $50 call at	$ 1.60
May 2008 $50 call at	$ .90
Total Value	$62.45 or 6.42 percent

(compared to the original cost of $58.68 on September 6, 2007)

Even with the HPQ stock down 7 percent, the value of the position on June 12, 2008, if liquidated, is up 6.42 percent. But even better, it is not possible to sustain a loss on this position. Between this point in time and January 17, 2009, the HPQ stock could go to zero and an exit value of $59.65 would be guaranteed. This guaranteed return is the result of the protective put option assuring a $50 sale price for the HPQ stock. On the other hand, the position can still increase dollar for dollar as the price of the HPQ moves over $50 between this point in time and the January 2009 expiration of the insurance. The upside for the stock is unlimited and we have already achieved a guaranteed $59.65 exit value with the potential for another 5 or 6 covered call writes that could be done to increase income and returns between now and expiration of the put option. As January approaches and the stock movement is strong, it is even possible to increase the strike price of the put option to lock in a greater profit. This strategy is flexible and allows the investor to implement different strategies depending on the actual stock movement — all from a position of a guaranteed return and with no downside risk.

IN CLOSING

Although these protective strategies can limit your maximum risk, it is always a good idea to have an exit strategy in place. In Chapter 7 we discussed the rules of thumb for rolling the married puts or long term debit collars if the stock moves down, but there is always a point where the ship has slipped too far beneath the waves. There are over 3,000 optionable stocks on the exchange. If the stock has stagnated for too long or dropped significantly in price, do not be afraid to liquidate the position or exercise the put option to exit the trade with a limited loss. Make sure you understand the specifics of these strategies and the total risks involved before you enter a trade. Options strategies involve risk and may not be suitable for all investors.

GLOSSARY

Action

Defines the type of trade the investor is entering. The standard actions when entering a trade are Buy to Open or Sell to Open. When closing a position, the standard actions are Buy to Close or Sell to Close.

Aggressive Investor

An investor that looks to trade positions with a high potential return, little or no protection, and a slim probability of earning the potential return.

All or None

A type of trade order that can be placed to assure the investor receives all shares or option contracts of a potential trade at a specific price set by the investor. If all shares or option contracts cannot be filled at the specific price, then no shares or option contracts will be traded.

American-Style Option

This kind of option contract may be exercised or assigned at any time between the date of purchase/write and the expiration date. Most exchange-traded options are American-style.

Ask Price

The price that sellers are trying to get for an equity or option on the open market. The ask price will usually be higher than the last trade price, since most investors are trying to sell at the highest price the market will support. The ask price is the most likely price a buyer will pay for an equity or option when placing a market order.

Assignment

The action an option seller encounters when the option buyer exercises their rights and the option seller has to fulfill their obligations. For a short call, assignment occurs when the call seller has to deliver shares of stock; for a short put, assignment occurs when the put seller is forced to buy shares of stock at the strike price.

At-the-Money (ATM)

An option whose strike price is equal to the price of its underlying stock. When the stock price is very close to the strike price, but not equal, it is said to be near-the-money. Near-the-money and at-the-money options tend to have the most time premium.

Average Stock Volume

The daily volume of shares traded for any stock averaged over the last 90 days.

Average Broker Recommendation

Zacks Investment Research firm's fundamental research provides data on brokers that rate companies from 1 to 5: 1 is a strong buy, 2 is a buy, 3 is a hold, 4 is a sell, and 5 is a strong sell recommendation. The average broker recommendation is the sum of all the recommendations divided by the number of brokers that have an opinion.

Back Testing

The practice of using historical data in order to analyze past performance of a particular trading methodology. The SmartHistoryXL tool mentioned in Chapter 4 is a useful tool for back testing options strategies.

Bearish Sentiment

The sentiment that a stock or the market in general will decline in price.

Bid Price

The price that buyers are trying to get for an equity or option on the open market. This price will usually be lower than the last trade price since buyers would like to pay the lowest amount possible for an equity or option. The bid price is the most likely price a seller will collect for an equity or option when placing a market order.

Bid-Ask Spread

The price spread between the bid price (what a seller is most likely to receive) and the ask price (what a buyer is most likely to pay) for an equity or an option. Both sellers and buyers will try to maximize their trades by entering a limit order for a value that is between the bid-ask spread.

Black-Scholes Model

The Black-Scholes Model is a theoretical pricing model for options developed by Fischer Black and Myron Scholes. It is based on 5 factors: (1) the underlying stock price; (2) the strike price of the option;

(3) days remaining to expiration; (4) current interest rates; and (5) the underlying stock volatility.

Black-Scholes Ratio

By comparing an option's Black-Scholes theoretical value to its current trading price, an investor can assess whether the option might be overvalued or undervalued. The B-S Ratio is calculated by taking the trading price of the option divided by the Black-Scholes theoretical worth for that option. Therefore, a B-S ratio of 1.2 tells us that the option is overvalued by 20 percent. A B-S Ratio of .8 tells us that the option is undervalued by 20 percent.

Break Even

The stock price at which any option strategy or combination stock and option strategy has a zero loss and a zero gain.

% to Break Even

The percentage a stock can change in value before the break even price is hit in any option strategy or combination stock and option strategy. For the married put strategy, the percent to break even is calculated by subtracting the current stock price from the break even price and then dividing that value by the current stock price.

Bullish Sentiment

The sentiment that a stock or the market in general will rise in price.

Buy and Hold

An investment strategy in which an investor will purchase stock, mutual funds or ETFs and hope that the underlying security rises in value over time so the investor realizes a profit.

Buy to Close

A type of investment action where an investor will buy back any option contracts that have been sold in order to cancel the fulfillment requirements or obligations.

Buy to Open

A type of investment action where an investor will buy into an equity or option contract to speculate on the movement of the underlying security.

Buyer

A purchaser or speculator of an equity or option contract.

Call Option

A contract that offers the owner the right, but not the obligation, to purchase stock at the strike price before the expiration date. One option contract gives the right to control 100 shares of the underlying stock until expiration unless the contract otherwise specifies.

Collar Spread Strategy

A neutral to bullish option investment strategy consisting of three legs: long stock, long a put option, and short a call option. The put option acts as insurance for the stock and the premium received from selling the call option lowers the cost of insurance. If the stock rises, the call may be assigned and the shares will be delivered at the call strike price.

Commissions

The price a broker will charge for an equity or option transaction.

Conservative Investor

An investor that looks to trade positions with a decent potential return, high protection, and a high probability of earning the potential return.

Conversion Spread

A type of collar spread in which the sold call and the long put have the same strike price. If a credit is received, the position can only profit by that amount but can never lose that amount. The profit and loss chart for a conversion spread is a straight line. Because the possibility of any reasonable returns is small, retail investors typically do not trade this strategy.

Cost of Insurance

Essentially, this is the time value of the put option. This is the total cost to the investor to own the protective put that acts as insurance for the stock.

Cost of Insurance per Day

The time value of the protective put option expressed against the days remaining until expiration. Protective put options that are far out in time will have a much lower cost of insurance per day.

Covered Call Strategy

A bullish investment strategy where a call option is sold against shares of stock that are owned in order to generate a cash income. For more information, refer to the Covered Call Help section on the PowerOptions website (www.poweropt.com).

Covered Position

An investment strategy where short call contracts are protected by ownership of an equal number of shares of the underlying security (covered call) or an equal number of purchased call contracts at a different strike (credit or debit spread); or, where short put contracts are protected by an equal number of short stock (covered put) or an equal number of purchased put contracts (credit or debit spread).

Credit Spread

An option investment strategy where an investor receives a credit for selling call or put options while buying an equal or different amount of call or put options on the same underlying security. If an investor sells call options and buys an equal number of call options at a higher strike price and receives a credit, the position is a bear call credit spread. If an investor sells put options and buys an equal number of put options at a lower strike price, the position is a bull put credit spread.

Day Order

A duration order that can be placed with a broker such that the order will remain open until fulfillment or until the end of the trading day the order was placed.

Debit Spread

An option investment strategy where an investor pays a debit for selling call or put options while buying an equal or different amount of call or put options on the same underlying security. If an investor sells call options and buys an equal number of call options at a lower strike price and pays a debit, the position is a bull call debit spread. If an investor sells put options and buys an equal number of put options at a higher strike price, the position is a bear put debit spread.

Delta

Delta is a measure of the sensitivity of the option value to changes in the underlying equity price. For every dollar of movement in the stock price, the price of the option can be expected to move by delta points. Puts have a negative delta. If the delta is -.5, then a one point increase in the underlying equity price will cause the put to lose $0.50 in value. A put option that is deep out-of-the-money (OTM) will have a delta close to zero. A put option that is deep in-the-money (ITM) will have a delta close to -1.

Earnings per Share Growth

Earnings per share growth is a company's change in earnings from last year to the estimate for the next year, divided by the earnings from last year, expressed as a percent. It is the expected earnings growth from year to year.

European Style

This kind of option contract may be exercised only during a specified period of time just prior to its expiration date.

Exercise

The action an option buyer takes to force the option seller to fulfill their obligations. When a call owner exercises their contract, the call owner will purchase shares of stock from the call seller. When a put owner exercises their contract, the put seller is forced to buy shares of stock.

Expiration Date

The date on which an option and the right to exercise it or have it assigned ceases to exist. For most equity options, the expiration date is the third Friday of the designated expiration month.

Expire (Worthless)

The action when an option is out-of-the-money (OTM) at expiration and ceases to exist without any intrinsic value.

Fundamental Criteria

The financial values of a stock that are used to determine the strength or weakness of the company. Some fundamental criteria include earnings, earnings growth, cash flow, and sales.

Future Expiration Value

The expected value of the equity or combination equity and option transaction at the expiration date, assuming the equity remains at the current value through expiration. This value is shown on the PowerOptions Profit/Loss Portfolio and Position Analysis tool for management calculations.

Gamma

The rate at which an options delta changes as the price of the underlying equity changes. Gamma is usually expressed in deltas gained or lost per a one point change in the underlying equity. As an example, if gamma is .05, the options delta would change .05 if the underlying equity moved one point.

Good Till Canceled

A duration order that can be placed with a broker such that the order will remain open until fulfillment or until canceled by the investor.

Greeks

Options criteria that measure how the instrument will change in price due to changes in the underlying equity, volatility of the stock, or interest rates in the market.

Implied Volatility

The stock volatility that is implied by the actual trading price of the option. The Black-Scholes model is used to back calculate what volatility must be to create the present price of the option.

Income Generating Strategy

Stock option investment strategy where a premium or credit is received on a regular basis. These include the naked put strategy, covered calls, credit spreads, and others.

Index Options

Option contracts that are available on an index such as the S&P 500 index, the Nasdaq 100 index, or the Russell 2000. Indexes represent a collection of various stocks and typically have a lower historical volatility because they do not fluctuate in price as frequently as individual stocks.

Institutional Holdings

The number of shares owned by organizations that primarily invest their own assets or on behalf of others. Some examples of institutional investors are employee pension funds, insurance companies, banks and university endowments.

In-the-Money (ITM)

This phrase describes the situation where the underlying stock price falls relative to the option strike price. A put option is in-the-money when the stock price is trading below the put strike price. A call option is in-the-money when the stock price is trading above the call strike price.

% In-the-Money

This is where the underlying stock price falls relative to the option strike price, expressed as a percentage. For a put option the % In-the-Money is calculated as:

% In-the-Money = (Put Strike Price – Stock Price) / Stock Price

Intrinsic Value

Every option premium is comprised of some intrinsic value and some time value. The intrinsic value is based on how deep in-the-money the stock is priced. For a put, it is how far below the strike price the stock price is located.

LEAPs

An acronym that stands for Long-term Equity Anticipation Securities. About 40% of the optionable stocks are available as LEAPS, and they are traded under different root symbols than the normal option series and only expire in January of the next two years. LEAPs is a registered trademark of the CBOE.

Limit Order

A type of order that is placed with the broker where the investor can set what price they would like to receive for selling or buying an equity or option. It is recommended to use a limit order when selling naked puts so the investor can hopefully receive a slightly higher premium than the offered bid price.

Liquidation Value

The value of an equity, option or combination equity and option strategy if the position were closed. This can be expressed as a monetary value or as a percentage.

Liquidity

A term used to describe how often an equity or option is traded. For options, liquidity can be measured using the volume of the option or the open interest.

Locked in Profit

The profit value that is guaranteed on a profitable stock position once a put option is purchased. At times the locked in profit might be lower than the unrealized gain, but once the put is in place, the return is guaranteed.

Long Position

When an investor is a holder of an equity or option position over a time when an increase in the price for the option or equity would be favorable. If an investor is long on a stock, they hope that the price goes up.

Long Call

A bullish strategy where the investor purchases a call option speculating on a rise in price of the underlying security, thus increasing the value of the purchased call.

Long Put

A bearish strategy where the investor purchases a put option speculating on a decrease in price of the underlying security, thus increasing the value of the purchased put.

Management Techniques

Methods that are used to help maximize the potential return or minimize the potential loss on an equity, option, or combination equity and option position.

Margin Requirement

The amount of money an uncovered (naked) option seller is required to deposit or have available in their account to maintain and cover an option position. Margin requirements are set separately by each brokerage house.

Market Capitalization

The stock price multiplied by the number of shares outstanding. A commonly used measure of the size of a company, since larger companies tend to have higher stock prices and a resultant higher number of stock splits.

Market Maker

An individual who sets the bid and ask prices for an equity or an option.

Market Order

A type of transaction order where the investor agrees to receive or pay the listed market price for an equity or option.

Married Put

A protective options investment strategy that consists of buying shares of stock and then purchasing a put option to protect the purchased shares.

Maximum Profit

The highest profit amount that can be made on the option position. For a married put trade the potential profits are unlimited. For a protective collar spread, the profits are limited by the sale of the short call option.

Maximum Risk

The highest value that can be lost on the option position. For the married put and collar spread strategy, the maximum risks are fairly low. The maximum risk for these strategies is defined as the total cost basis minus the strike price of the put option.

Moderate Investor

An investor that looks to trade positions where some protection is forfeited for a slightly higher return, with a 50-50 chance of earning the return.

Naked Call

A bearish strategy where the investor realizes a profit by making cash from selling (writing) a call without having the cash investment of owning the stock as in a covered call strategy. While the stock goes down, the investor keeps the premium on the sold call.

Naked Put

A bullish strategy where the investor realizes a profit by making cash from selling (writing) a put without having the cash investment of shorting the stock as in a covered put strategy. While the stock goes up, the investor keeps the premium on the sold put.

Net Debit

The total cost to the investor when entering a long position. For married puts, the net debit is the cost of the stock plus the cost of the put option. For a collar spread, the net debit is the cost of the stock plus the cost of the put option minus the call premium received.

Neutral Sentiment

The sentiment that a stock or the market in general will remain in a sideways trading range over a period of time.

Open Interest

Open interest represents the number of open option contracts on the market over the life of the contract. The open interest is a measure of how liquid the options' contracts can be. When there is little or no open interest for an option, it can still be liquid because the Options Clearing Corporation (OCC) will make a market for it.

Option

A derivative investment vehicle that is a contract to purchase or sell shares of the underlying stock. There are two types of options, calls and puts.

Option Chain

A tool that allows investors to view various data points for all call and put options that are available on an underlying equity.

Option Series

The available option expiration months that an investor can use to sell or buy options on a given equity. There are three option series: JAJO (January, April, July, October), MJSD (March, June, September, December), and FMAN (February, May, August, November). Every optionable stock will have the near and next month expiration available.

Option Symbol

An option symbol is comprised of three parts. The first one to three letters are the root symbol for the option. The second to last letter stands for the expiration month of the contract. The last letter in the symbol represents the strike price for the contract.

Option Volume

Option volume is the number of contracts traded on the current trading session or on the last trading day in the case of a holiday when the market is closed. Both buy orders and sell orders will cause this characteristic to increase.

Order Duration

A specification placed with your broker to cancel the trade or leave it open based on the time frame you selected. Some examples include Day Order, Good 'Till Canceled, and Immediate or Cancel.

Order Type

A specification placed with your broker allowing an investor to select how they want the position to be filled. Some examples include market order and limit order.

Out-of-the-Money (OTM)

This phrase describes the situation where the underlying stock price falls relative to the option strike price. A put option is out-of-the-money when the stock price is trading above the put strike price. A call option is out-of-the-money when the stock price is trading below the call strike price.

% Out-of-the-Money

This is where the underlying stock price falls relative to the option strike price, expressed as a percentage. For a put option the % Out-of-the-Money is calculated as:

% Out-of-the-Money = (Stock Price − Put Strike Price) / Stock Price

Paper Trade

A useful educational method an investor can use before placing any actual trades. Paper trading with tools such as the PowerOptions Portfolio will help investors gain confidence and understanding of the market before placing real trades.

Premium

Another term for the price of the option.

Price-to-Earnings Ratio
The stock price divided by last year's earnings. The higher the P/E ratio, the more you are paying for each dollar of earnings.

Probability Above/Below
This is the theoretical chance that an option has of being assigned. Specifically, it is the chance that the stock price will be above or below the strike of the option. This is commonly expressed as a percentage.

Protective Put
A protective investment strategy where an investor will purchase put options to protect their shares of stock from large declines. The put acts as insurance for the underlying equity.

Put Option
A contract that gives the owner the right, but not the obligation, to sell a stock at the strike price before the expiration date. One option contract gives the right to control 100 shares of stock until expiration, unless the contract otherwise specifies.

% Return if Assigned
The percentage return that is achieved in the collar spread strategy when the stock is trading above the strike price of the sold call and the stock is assigned. This return takes into account the premium that is received and any profit/loss between the stock price and the sold call strike price, as well as the theoretical value remaining on the long put.

% Return if Assigned (Annualized)
The % return if assigned value multiplied by 365, divided by the number of days remaining to the sold options expiration.

Rho

A measure of the sensitivity of an option's price to a change in interest rates.

Risk-Reward Chart

A graphical interpretation of the maximum profit and potential losses for a given investment strategy.

Risk-Reward Ratio

A ratio of the various risk, risk-aversion, and reward values for a given investment strategy.

Roll Down

The process of closing a current option position or letting it expire, then opening a new position at a lower strike price for the current expiration month or further out in time.

Roll Out

The process of closing a current option position or letting it expire, then opening a new position at the same strike, one expiration month or more out in time.

Roll Up

The process of closing a current option position or letting it expire, then opening a new position at a higher strike price for the current expiration month or further out in time.

Sell to Close

A type of investment action where an investor will sell any long option contracts in order to cancel the fulfillment requirements or obligations.

Sell to Open

A type of investment action where an investor will sell any option contracts in order to cancel the fulfillment requirements or obligations.

Seller

A seller (writer) of an equity or option contract.

Short Position

When an investor is a seller of an equity or option position over a time when a decrease in the price for the option or equity would be favorable. If an investor is short on a stock, they hope that the price goes down.

Simple Moving Average

Moving averages can be used to gauge the direction of price movement in any stock. They are typically measured in 20, 50, 100, 200, or 250 day ranges. For married puts and collar spread trades, an investor might want to look for stocks that are trading above their 20 day or 50 day moving averages (currently in an uptrend).

Stop Loss

A type of order that can be placed with a broker to help an investor manage their positions. A stop loss will trigger a closing action on the open position if a target price is encountered.

Strike Price

The price at which an option owner has the right, but not the obligation to buy shares of stock (in the case of a call option) or sell shares of stock (in the case of a put option); and the price at which an option seller must deliver shares of stock (in the case of a short call option) or buy shares of stock (in the case of a short put option).

Technical Criteria

Stock analysis criteria that is based on the movements and trends of the stock and usually interpreted through charts.

Theoretical Value (Option)

The fair market value of an option determined using a theoretical calculation such as the Black-Scholes pricing model. By comparing the actual trading price of an option to its theoretical value, an investor can determine if the option is overvalued or undervalued.

Theta (Time Decay Factor)

The rate at which an option loses value as time passes. An option with a theta of $0.04 will lose $0.04 in value for each passing day. Therefore, if the option is worth $2.73 today, then tomorrow it will be worth $2.69 and the day after it will be worth $2.65.

Time Value or % Time Value

Every option premium is made up of some time value and some intrinsic value. From its creation date to its expiration date, an option's time value decays away and any value left is intrinsic value, which rises or falls with the price of the stock. The percent time value is the time value shown as a percent of the stock price.

Uncovered Position

An option position where stock has not been purchased or shorted to cover a sold call or a sold put. Uncovered positions are typically referred to as naked positions.

Underlying Security

The equity (either stock, index or ETF) whose shares are represented by the option contract that has been sold or purchased.

Vega (Kappa)

The sensitivity of an option's theoretical value to a change in volatility. If an option has a vega of $0.13, for each percentage point increase in volatility, the option will gain $0.13 in value. As an example, if the value of the option is $3.50 at a volatility of 30 percent, then it will have a theoretical value of $3.63 at a volatility of 31 percent and a value of $3.37 at a volatility of 29 percent.

Volatility

A statistical measure of the annual fluctuation of the underlying stock. The volatility is used in option pricing models to determine the fair value of an option. Generally, the higher an equity's volatility, the more inflated the underlying option bid prices will be. Volatility is one of the factors considered in the Black-Scholes theoretical option pricing model. Several time periods can be used to create this measure. The standard volatility that is shown on PowerOptions is the 50 day volatility.

Volume

The total number of shares traded on a stock or the total number of contracts traded on an option for a given day.

Write

Another term that is used to describe when an option is sold. Option sellers are also referred to as "option writers."

ERNIE ZERENNER

During a 30 year career at Hewlett-Packard, Ernie Zerenner forged a trail of achievement. He developed four patents, delivered six well-received papers, received an international award for his invention of the Fused Silica Column, and had an impressive list of industry firsts, including the first microprocessor-driven instrument in the analytical industry.

During his tenure, Ernie continued his lifelong fascination with the stock market, building a successful portfolio. When retirement loomed, Ernie felt it was necessary to switch his investing philosophy from seeking capital gains to creating income from assets owned. So he turned to covered calls, an options trading strategy designed to generate consistent income.

Using a calculator and the financial pages, it took eight to ten hours to find good opportunities. In an attempt to cut that time frame, Ernie teamed with a colleague to design a program to scan the entire market and find the best covered calls. The time required to do the job dropped from eight hours to eight minutes. It was breakthrough technology that earned a patent, and was the basis for a web site called PowerOpt.com, which now not only supports Ernie's covered call investments, but thousands of subscriber/investors in, at last count, 57 countries all over the world.

PowerOpt.com is still the largest subscription program of Power Financial Group, the trading company Ernie established in 1997. Today, he continues to innovate and seek ways to help investors grow through options trading.

MICHAEL CHUPKA

Michael Chupka grew up in northern Delaware, his father a Ph.D. in chemistry and mother a registered nurse. In his high school years, Michael was deeply involved with various service organizations, mainly Key Club, giving much of his time freely to others. He also worked part-time as a manager of a local store between his obligations as an officer of Key Club and captain of the cross country team.

Michael attended the University of Missouri-Rolla, majoring in geology, micro-paleontology, and English literature. He left University of Missouri-Rolla and returned to Delaware with hopes to further pursue his studies in the field of paleo-biology.

It was during this time that Power Financial Group, Inc., was in the midst of a major growth period and was looking to expand its support team. Greg Zerenner, Vice President of PowerOptions and now President of PowerOptionsApplied, approached Michael with an opportunity to join the PowerOptions staff. It was Mr. Zerenner's idea that Michael's strong dedication to service combined with a knowledge of scientific methods would make him a perfect fit to the PowerOptions support team.

Five years and tens of thousands of PowerOptions customers later, Mr. Chupka has established himself as head of the PowerOptions support team and a recognized options strategy educator in the industry. Michael has written dozens of educational articles for PowerOptions, and this is Michael's second book co-authored with Ernie Zerenner, President of Power Financial Group, Inc..

TRADING
RESOURCE
GUIDE

RECOMMENDED READING

THE FOUR BIGGEST MISTAKES IN OPTION TRADING, 2ND EDITION

by Jay Kaeppel

With over 50,000 copies in print for the first edition, Kaeppel's insight has undoubtedly made its mark in the options world. Now, he strikes again with an updated and more comprehensive look at those pesky mistakes that traders continue to make in trading options. In easy-to-understand terms, he systematically breaks down each problem and offers concrete and practical solutions to overcome it in the future.

Item #BCPOx4941403 • List Price: $19.95

OPTION VOLATILITY TRADING STRATEGIES

by Sheldon Natenberg

Unlike price and time, volatility is the one element of the market that is virtually invisible to a trader. Thus, having accurate methods to assess this elusive aspect is critical to successful options trading. With advances in technology, options have swelled in popularity and traders have risked their fortunes without an easy-to-understand explanation of the important factors in separating profit from loss.

Now, presented with clear and understandable insight are option-trading strategies, formulas, and definitions. You'll feel as if the master of trading, Sheldon Natenberg, is right next to you, guiding you through this potentially complex world of options.

Item #BCPOx5127729 • List Price: $39.95

MAKE MONEY TRADING: HOW TO BUILD A WINNING TRADING BUSINESS

by Jean Folger & Lee Leibfarth

Want to be your own boss? Live independently? Take a more active role in managing your money?

That's what a trading business can mean for you -- money, independence, and complete control over your finances. But without the proper education, about 90% of people will fail. That's why this book is essential to your trading success.

Item #BCPOx5312378 • List Price: $29.95

OPTION TRADING TACTICS COURSE BOOK WITH DVD

by Oliver L. Velez

In this unique DVD/course book package, you'll learn Velez's secrets to enhancing your trading skills through options. It includes a full-length DVD of Velez's famed *Options Trading Seminar* and a corresponding course book to ensure you have all the tools necessary to make money with options.

Item #BCPOx5440077 • List Price: $39.95

▲ ▲ ▲ ▲ ▲ ▲

To get the current lowest price on any item listed
Go to www.traderslibrary.com

THE LEAPS STRATEGIST: 108 PROVEN STRATEGIES FOR INCREASING INVESTMENT & TRADING PROFITS

by Michael C. Thomsett

Unleash the power of Long-Term Equity Anticipation Securities (LEAPS) for increasing gains, limiting losses, and protecting your trading and investing profits. The 108 powerful strategies lined out in this comprehensible guide by author Michael C. Thomsett help you both to advance your investing and trading techniques and to achieve your financial goals. Real-world examples and graphic illustrations point out the main keys of this book. Not only are LEAPS a low-risk alternative to buying stock, they are also a great way to maximize your capital.

Item #BCPOx2529875 • List Price: $34.95

NAKED PUTS: POWER STRATEGIES FOR CONSISTENT PROFITS

by Ernie Zerenner and Michael Chupka

In the first book in the Power Options series, Ernie Zerenner and Michael Chupka take on the topic of naked puts. You may have heard rumors that trading naked puts is risky, but these two prove that the rumors are outdated and the reality is that naked puts have the same risk-reward tolerance as covered calls, one of the most conservative of trading strategies. The naked put position allows an investor to take advantage of a neutral to bullish market sentiment without actually buying shares of stock. With helpful tips on using Power Options software, you'll feel like you're getting a personal lesson from these experts.

Item #BCPOx5501177 • List Price: $19.95

PowerOptions Products and Services for all Investors!

For Self Directed Investors

POWEROptions®
www.poweropt.com

* Patented search tools in over 23 different option strategies.
* Volumes of education and tips.
* Paper trading, tracking and management tools.
* Back testing tools for each strategy.
* Find the best trades to meet your preferences.

Not Self Directed?

POWEROptionsApplied
www.poweroptionsapplied.com

* We pick the trades and tell you when to close or roll the position.
* Several TradeFolios to meet your needs.
* Make money in all market conditions.
* Up-to-the-minute tracking and trading info.

Are you still in the learning process? Let our experience help you!

Covered Call Course
www.poweropt.com/ccoffer.asp

* Details Ernie and Greg Zerenner's covered call methodologies.
* Learn to generate consistent income trading covered calls with confidence.
* Kit includes book, dvd and workbook filled with charts, graphs and information.
* Receive 2 free months of PowerOptions when you purchase the kit, a $180 value!!!

PowerOptions Trading Series
www.poweropt.com/products.asp

* Detailed texts for various options strategies with a focus on using PowerOptions tools.
* Benefit from the author's combined 35 + years of trading experience.
* Chapters walk you through the strategy from beginning to end; start with the basics and move to advanced management techniques.
* Low cost and loaded with information!!!

Marketplace **Books** is the preeminent publisher of trading, investing, and finance educational material. We produce professional books, DVDs, courses, and electronic books (ebooks) that showcase the exceptional talent working in the investment world today. Started in 1993, Marketplace Books grew out of the realization that mainstream publishers were not meeting the demand of the trading and investment community. Capitalizing on the access we had through our distribution partner Traders' Library, Marketplace Books was launched, and today publishes the top authors in the industry—household names like Jack Schwager, Oliver Velez, Larry McMillan, Sheldon Natenberg, Jim Bittman, Martin Pring, and Jeff Cooper are just the beginning. We are actively acquiring some of the brightest new minds in the industry including technician Jeff Greenblatt and programmers Jean Folger and Lee Leibfarth.

From the beginning student to the professional trader, our goal is to continually provide the highest quality resources for those who want an active role in the world of finance. Our products focus on strategic information and cutting edge research to give our readers the best education possible. We are at the forefront of digital publishing and are actively pursuing innovative ways to deliver content. At our annual Traders' Forum event, our readers get the chance to learn and mingle with our top authors in a way unprecedented in the industry. Our titles have been translated in most major world languages and can be shipped all over the globe thanks to our preferred online bookstore, TradersLibrary.com.

Visit us today at:

www.marketplacebooks.com & www.traderslibrary.com

This book, and other great products, are available at significantly discounted prices. They make great gifts for your customers, clients, and staff. For more information on these long-lasting, cost-effective premiums, please call (800) 272-2855, or email us at sales@traderslibrary.com.